Tolkien in East Y
1917 - 1918

An Illustrated Tour

Phil Mathison

Published by Dead Good Publications
Newport,
East Yorkshire
HU15 2RF

Front cover
Southern approach to Dents Garth from the west side of
Roos All Saints' Church

Rear cover
The site of Monkwith, one of the many lost villages of Holderness
A classic view of this rapidly eroding coastline

OTHER TITLES BY THE AUTHOR

Shed Bashing with the The Beatles (ISBN 9780954693732)
The Spurn Gravel Trade (ISBN 9780954693763)
The Saint of Spurn Point (ISBN 9780956299406)

ISBN 978-0-9562994-1-3

Published by Dead Good Publications
Newport,
East Yorkshire
HU15 2RF

Contents

Foreword

Even within the East Riding of Yorkshire, there are relatively few people who realise that J R R Tolkien spent time in the area during World War 1. Fewer still recognise the influence that their locality had on the writings of this giant of 20th century literature. Over several years, I have researched the author's residence here, hopefully separating the myth and rumour from the facts. I have pursued the matter more as a piece of detective work, coupled with my life long love of the area, than the creation of a literary tour de force. This small tome is the result of my endeavours. Wherever possible, primary sources have been used to substantiate any claims made for specific locations identified herein. This publication does not claim to be the last word on the matter, for even at this remove of time, some unknown source may surface to illuminate was has been invisible up until now. If anyone does have any snippet of relevant information, then I would be delighted to hear from them.

The book is profusely illustrated, as I wanted to bring this corner of England to the attention of a wider audience, and particularly to individuals who appreciate the inherent beauty and richness of an English shire steeped in history. The towns and villages portrayed within these pages are my villages and towns, and they are like old friends to me, having lived in the area since birth sixty years ago. Indeed Holderness, that is, the area bounded in the west by the River Hull, in the east by the North Sea, and to the north by Driffield and Bridlington, is one of my favourite areas of Great Britain. It is a sleepy backwater, a largely unspoilt gem of rural England, and long may it remain so. Unless credited otherwise, all photographs were taken by me.

This book would not have been possible without the assistance of a number of people. First and foremost is John Garth, who has kindly given me permission to reproduce some of the information from his book entitled 'Tolkien and the Great War – The Threshold of Middle-earth'. From the beginning, John has been patient, helpful and informative, even when faced with a barrage of queries from a Tolkien novice like me! References to the literary ideas being crafted by JRRT while he was recuperating in 1917 and 1918 are largely derived from his excellent and thoroughly researched publication, which is highly recommended to any serious student of this great author. I would like to thank Charles Noad of the Tolkien Society for being my first point of contact on the topic, and for facilitating the initial introduction to John Garth. Wayne Hammond and Christina Scull, acknowledged experts on Tolkien, took the time and trouble via E-mail to assist me, and kindly gave me permission to reproduce some snippets from their 2 volume publication 'JRR Tolkien Companion and Guide'. It is a masterpiece of research, and a treasure trove of useful information. Both 'Tolkien and the Great War – The Threshold of Middle-earth' and 'JRR Tolkien Companion and Guide' are published by HarperCollins. I would like to take this opportunity to thank HarperCollins for their kind permission to make reference to both these excellent publications in these pages. The primary source for the addresses listed in the book was the Tolkien archive at the Bodleian Library at Oxford. Therefore, I am deeply indebted to Cathleen Blackburn of the Tolkien Estate lawyer, Maier Blackburn of Oxford, who patiently fielded my time consuming questions with alacrity. In turn, the poor archivist, Catherine Parker, had to dig and provide Cathleen with the necessary information. Many thanks go to both these ladies for their generous assistance. Next I would like to thank my wife, Mary, who had the tedious job of listening to my ramblings on the matter, being my companion as I visited the locations, and then had the unenviable task of proof reading my deliberations. The National Archives at Kew are a real treasure, and what an amazing resource they were when Mary and I visited them in August 2011 to inspect the original War Office records. Thanks go to the Powys County Archive for the Owen Ashton connection. The staff at Beverley Treasure House have, as always, been patient and extremely helpful on my numerous visits to this well stocked archive. The Hull History Centre has likewise proved invaluable at points in my research. On my travels, Tony Simpson and James Maxwell of the Withernsea Lighthouse Museum have always been ready to help me, and initially put me on the track of the Gilbert Mackereth connection.

Terry Dean in Lancashire has been extremely generous with his time in matters relating to the Lancashire Fusiliers, and thanks must go to the Sloan family for allowing the use of the Thirtle Bridge and Sand-le-Mere images. The staff at Endsleigh Convent were very welcoming, and my conversation with Sister Agnes in August 2011, who met Sister Mary Michael in 1947, was one of the highlights of my research. Sister Barbara at the Institute of Our Lady of Mercy Archive in London is to be congratulated on finding the photograph of Sister Mary Michael. As always, Jan Crowther of Kilnsea has assisted with details, and Tony Ellis of Tunstall Hall provided me with the fact that his home had been officer's quarters in the last century. Elaine Dunn, and Stewart Hodgson of Mona House, Thirtle Bridge, have helped where they can with the Thirtle Bridge site that surrounds their home, and I thank Stewart for permission to reproduce his sketch map of what remained of the camp in the 1950s. Additionally, Stuart Smales of Renish Farm helped with some details of the camp, and allowed me to walk on his land and photograph Tunstall Drain. Paul Sullivan of Hornsea Lakes Premier Holiday Park kindly allowed me to take photographs on the site of the former Rolston Rifle Range. I wish to thank Stella Morris for permission to read the Walker diaries of Easington during the Great War and reproduce them here. Cheryl Jones, General Manager of the Holderness Gazette, has always been supportive and offered advice when needed. Peter Cook of Withernsea offered me tit-bits about locations in

Roos rumoured to have Tolkien connections. I am sure that there are other individuals who have contributed, and I hope that they will forgive me for forgetting their names. Trust me, any help with my research, no matter how small, has been greatly appreciated, and I hope that the end result presented here is some small recompense for any input I have received from many people over the years.

Phil Mathison
April 2012

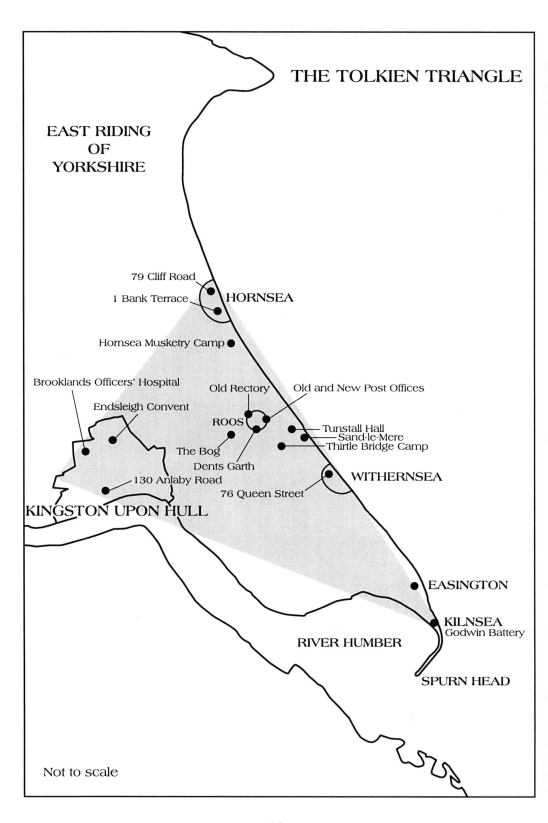

THE TOLKIEN TRIANGLE

EAST RIDING
OF
YORKSHIRE

79 Cliff Road

1 Bank Terrace · HORNSEA

Hornsea Musketry Camp ●

Brooklands Officers' Hospital

Old Rectory   Old and New Post Offices

Endsleigh Convent

ROOS

Tunstall Hall
Sand-le-Mere
Thirtle Bridge Camp

The Bog

Dents Garth

130 Anlaby Road

WITHERNSEA

KINGSTON UPON HULL

76 Queen Street

EASINGTON

KILNSEA
Godwin Battery

RIVER HUMBER

SPURN HEAD

Not to scale

Why Tolkien was in East Yorkshire

In the 21st Century there can be few people in the world who do not recognise the name of John Ronald Reuel Tolkien. Many will have read the author's excellent books, and others in recent years will have been entertained and enthralled by the epic films directed by Peter Jackson. However, in 1917, JRRT was just another officer in His Majesty's forces, recently graduated from Oxford. He had enlisted in his university town on June 28th 1915, and was given a commission on July 15th as a 2nd Lieutenant, subsequently joining the 13th service Battalion Lancashire Fusiliers. It is ironic, in the light of Tolkien's subsequent travels, that this unit had been formed at Hull in December 1914. However, Tolkien did not fight in this unit, as it was a draft-finding unit only. He subsequently underwent training, which included a spell at the Army's Northern Command at Farnley Park, Otley, Yorkshire in April 1916 (1).

He went out to France on June 6th 1916, and served in the 11th Battalion of the Lancashire Fusiliers. Having seen action, he was taken ill and diagnosed with trench fever at Beauval on October 27th. The following day he left the 11th Battalion of the Lancashire Fusiliers, and after a stay in hospital in Le Touquet, he departed the shores of France for Blighty on November 8th, on the hospital ship 'Asturias' from Le Havre. The next day he arrived at Birmingham University Hospital, in Edgbaston, and officially known as the First Southern General Hospital. It is at this point that a future posting to Yorkshire becomes a possibility. A letter of November 27th from the headquarters of the 3rd (Reserve) Battalion of the Lancashire Fusiliers, to the hospital at Edgbaston, states 'you will issue orders for 2nd Lieutenant J R R Tolkien, 11th Battalion Lancashire Fusiliers'. The communication adds 'at an early date' (2). So Tolkien was expected in Yorkshire, as soon as possible, by the 3rd (Reserve) Battalion of the Lancashire Fusiliers, to assist with their defence of the east coast. At this time their H.Q was based at Ottringham, a Holderness village some fourteen miles east of Hull, although the 1916 Lancashire Fusiliers Annual gives the location as Halsham, which is two miles to the north.

However, before his eventual arrival in Yorkshire, he attended a military medical board on December 2nd, and they sent him home to Great Haywood, near Stafford, for several weeks. In January 1917 he was ready for duty once more but attendance at another medical board on January 23rd showed a recurrence of the fever and he returned home for a further period of leave. He attended a further medical board on February 27th at Lichfield but was found to be little improved. As Edith and his cousin Jennie Grove had taken lodgings in Harrogate, Tolkien left the West Midlands and went to stay with them. He attended yet another medical board on March 28th at Furness Auxiliary Hospital. The report noted 'He is improving. He still complains of pains in his knees and elbows'. He was considered unfit for general and home service for one month but fit for one month's light duty at home, and a further three week's sick leave was recommended. It then goes on to mention his scheduled dispatch, when ready, to the 3rd Battalion Lancashire Fusiliers at Withernsea.

During his stay in Harrogate, Tolkien was visited by Christopher Luke Wiseman, one of three other chums who in their youth had formed a group called the Tea Club and Barrovian Society. Two other members, Robert Quilter Gilson and Geoffrey Bache Smith, were already war fatalities, and so it was a much diminished society that celebrated the 'Council of Harrogate' on April 18th 1917. Wiseman was pleased that JRRT was still recuperating, for it kept him in England, and away from the fighting. However, the following day, Tolkien was thrown back into military life, for he was sent to the Humber Garrison. Initially the posting was to the 3rd Lancashire Fusiliers' outpost and musketry school at Hornsea, but at last the author had arrived in the northern shire that was to be his home and inspiration for the next eighteen months.

The covering letter for Tolkien's Medical Board, dated May 1st 1917, showing their address as 130 Anlaby Road, Hull. (Courtesy of the National Archives, Kew)

130, Anlaby Road,
Hull,
1/5/17

The Secretary,
War Office,
London, S.W.

Sir,

I have the honour to forward herewith original proceedings of Medical Board held this day on the under-mentioned Officer.

2/Lt. J.R.R. Tolkien, 11 attch 3 Lan. Fus.

I have the honour to be,
Sir,
Your obedient servant.

Lt. Col., R.A.M.C.
P.M.O.
HUMBER GARRISON.

Kingston upon Hull

It is here that we must backtrack, and start our geographical tour of the East Riding of Yorkshire at this great port on the River Humber. Hull, even today, has been described as being at the end of a fifty mile cul-de-sac. It is a city a visitor has to go to, rather than passing through to some other place, unless that some other place is Europe via the ferry. Chronologically, Tolkien's first posting was to Hornsea, but he would have arrived at the seaside resort via the services of the North Eastern Railway into Hull Paragon Station. There he would have changed trains to travel on the branch line to his final destination at the coastal town. I list the chronological events relevant to JRRT's stay in East Yorkshire later in the book.

As a city, Kingston upon Hull was a major shipping, fishing and industrial centre, but unfortunately, being on the east coast of England, it was also within reach of Germany. During World War 1, the conurbation was attacked a number of times by zeppelins, and it was the constant threat of bombardment and invasion that necessitated the formation of defences in the locality. To this end, the Humber Garrison was instituted, with camps all along the Holderness coast, and especially near the mouth of the River Humber at Kilnsea and Spurn Point.

The start of our Tolkien tour finds us at the site of 130 Anlaby Road, Hull, the home of the Medical Board of the Humber Garrison. The 1892 Ordnance Survey map called the row of houses here Tremayne Terrace, but this title had vanished by World War 1. The building has long gone, and the whole area is now a car park, graced by a derelict petrol station immediately to the west. It is situated on the north side of Anlaby Road, about a quarter of a mile west of Paragon Station. In the 1914 and 1915 Kelly's Local Directories, John Blackbourn, a bone setter lived there. The entry disappears in the 1916 and 1919 directories, probably due to wartime censorship of anything military, but reappears in 1921 with a certain George Henry Jefferson, a dealer in hay, etc., now in residence. It is here that we enter the area of conjecture, for the National Archive has eight relevant documents from the records of the Medical Board. All are covering letters that would have been attached to Tolkien's Medical Board reports. They are dated May 1st 1917, June 1st 1917, October 16th 1917, November 16th 1917, February 19th 1918, July 17th 1918, September 4th 1918 and September 8th 1918 (3). Only on October 16th 1917 and the last three dates was the writer actually based in Hull. On the other occasions he was stationed at camps on the Holderness coast. This begs the question – did he travel into Hull on the dates recorded, to attend these medicals, or were they conducted at the camps, and the paperwork forwarded to the War Office in London courtesy of the Humber Garrison Medical

H.Q. on Anlaby Road? We shall never know. It would be logical for the examinations to take place in situ, removing the expense and inconvenience of soldiers travelling into Hull. The completed report could then be sent to the H.Q. for forwarding to the Capital. Despite the obvious advantage of such a procedure, knowing the bureaucratic nature of the armed forces, I feel it probable that Tolkien did actually visit Anlaby Road on several occasions to be examined by an independent practitioner. The military may have assumed, probably rightly, that any man examined at his base camp might try to sway the decision of the incumbent doctor, who may even have been a friend and comrade. If this had been the case, then JRRT must have had to arrange transport to the nearest railhead, be it Hornsea or Withernsea, and thence by train into Hull Paragon station.

Our second destination in the city is Brooklands Military Hospital. By comparing the 1910 and present day Ordnance Survey maps, I was able to deduce that the building is now called The Dennison Centre, Cottingham Road, and is the home of the University of Hull's International Office, but back in 1917 it was a hospital under the jurisdiction of Mrs Strickland Constable (4). In 1912, according to the Kelly's Directory, Robert Foster lived in the imposing edifice. Again, the address disappears in the directories for 1914, 1915 and 1919, for obvious reasons, and resurfaces in 1921. By then it was the residence of Alfred

Ernest Thomas, a managing director, who would have been blissfully unaware of the earlier stay by the author who was to bring the world 'The Hobbit' within twenty years. Tolkien had two lengthy stays in the place, from mid-August 1917 to mid-October, and then again from June 29th 1918 to October 11th, when he departed the establishment for the delights of the Savoy Convalescent Hospital at Blackpool on the Lancashire coast, where he stayed until the war was over.

It is no surprise that hospitals feature in the writer's military life at this time, for the effects of the trench fever could last for many months. Therefore, it was a recurrence of this condition that brought him to Cottingham Road. While he was invalided there, the city experienced a zeppelin raid, but this did not disrupt the hospital and Tolkien found the place quite conducive to his creativity. The atmosphere was convivial, and he even had a regimental friend (whose name is unknown to us) for company (5). Cottingham Road was, and is, a wide leafy avenue, and at that time it was near the northern reaches of the city, and would probably have had a rural vista directly to the north.

During his initial stay, Tolkien wrote his poem 'Companions of the Rose' (still unpublished), which was dedicated to Robert Quilter Gilson and Geoffrey Bache Smith, the two deceased members of the Tea Club & Barrovian Society. The title refers to the white rose that is worn on August 1ˢᵗ by their two regiments, the Lancashire Fusiliers (Tolkien and Smith) and the Suffolks (Gilson) to commemorate Minden Day, the date of a regimental triumph in 1688. He forwarded the completed work to Wiseman, who liked it, and in one letter commented that the writer seemed to have 'spent a good time on the mythology'. Of course, Wiseman was referring to the mythical world that Tolkien was even then conjuring up with his amazing imagination. Early in 1917 the story of Tinuviel and Beren (part of which Aragorn recounts to his hobbit companions on Weathertop in 'The Fellowship of the Ring') was taking shape, eventually to become part of the 'Lost Tales'. Further input was undertaken while JRRT was convalescing at Brooklands Hospital. Indeed, work on the 'Lost Tales' continued incrementally all the time that Tolkien was in residence at Brooklands. The Lost Tales was rewritten and revised over and over again throughout Tolkien's life, but appeared in print posthumously as 'The Silmarillion'. As to the 'Tale of Turambar', another story on which he was working during this period, it is worth noting that one of the lost villages of the Holderness coast was called Turmarr, and was situated near Easington, a location to which Tolkien was later posted. Also, about five miles north of Roos, near Garton, is a farm called Turmar Farm, and he could well have passed this on the journey from Hornsea to Thirtle Bridge, which are both locations with which his name is associated. Is it possible, that in the author's mind, the name of this vanished hamlet was refashioned into the very similar 'Turambar'? Further revision was done on his poem 'The Mermaid's Flute', and 'The Grey Bridge at Tavrobel' (which is believed to allude to Great Haywood) also saw the first light of day while he was convalescing at Brooklands, for a written note on the poem states 'August / September 1917'. Tolkien was still labouring with the poem 'Sea Chant of an Elder Day', and about this time he re-titled it 'The Horns of Ulmo' He noted that the 'Present shape was due to rewriting and adding an introduction in a lonely house near Roos, Holderness.' This of course alludes to his stay at Thirtle Bridge earlier in the year, but more of that later.

Tolkien's wife, Edith, was staying at Withernsea when he first went into Brooklands Hospital, and probably visited him there several times by catching the Hull train, and travelling the two miles to Cottingham Road by omnibus or walking. However, she sent her last letter from the seaside to him on August 21st, and returned south, presumably with Jennie Grove, to accommodation in Cheltenham, from where she wrote to him on August 24th(6). She would have passed through Hull on her train journey from the seaside resort, and we can safely assume that she would have visited her husband at that time, probably on August 22nd or 23rd. The correspondence continued from Cheltenham until October 15th. The Humber Garrison Medical Board, reporting on October 16th 1917 noted 'He has been in

Brooklands Officers' Hospital for past 9 weeks. It is now 3 weeks since his temperature reached normal. He has not yet recovered his strength – He still suffers from debility and pain in arms and shins and looks delicate.' He was rated 30% disabled, but told to rejoin the 3rd Lancs. Fus. at Thirtle Bridge, having been found fit for light duties at home (7). Discharged from the hospital, he returned to his battalion at Thirtle Bridge. At Cottingham Road for the second time towards the end of June 1918, Tolkien occupied himself with further work on the languages he was inventing to support the mythology he was creating. The speech of Elves was starting to take shape, with the Finnish language influencing Qenya, and Goldogrin inspired by Tolkien's love of Welsh (8). Despite this absorption with his invented tongues, he also found time to improve his knowledge of some actual languages, Spanish and Italian, and even began to acquire some Russian! He received orders to proceed to France via Boulogne on July 26th, which totally overlooked the fact that he was in a military hospital! Fortunately, the order was countermanded on July 31st. However, unfortunately, his general health was severely compromised, as the report of The Medical Board at the Humber Garrison of September 4th 1918 recorded (9). It stated that Tolkien had been at Brooklands Officers' Hospital, since June 29th, having contracted gastritis at Brocton Camp, Staffs. The report then continues 'During his stay in hospital he has made some progress. He has lost nearly 2 stone but is gradually regaining weight. He is only on restricted diet. He is recommended to transfer (sic) to Convalescent Hospital'. The board considered him 100% disabled and unfit in any category for two months, and is instructed to remain in the hospital for that period. By now he is 26 years old, and has served in the Army for three years and two months, of which two years and eight months have been in England and six months have been abroad.'

The author's invalidity in a strange town, and his Catholic faith, lead us to the third Hull connection – the Convent of Mercy. While in Brooklands Military Hospital, Tolkien, presumably like many other patients, was visited by the Sisters of Mercy. Founded by Venerable Catherine McAuley in Dublin in 1831, the Sisters of Mercy arrived in Kingston upon Hull in 1857, initially to Dansom Lane / Wilton Street (10). By 1873 the Sisters had a purpose-built convent on Anlaby Road, between Convent Lane and South Parade. This is interesting, for the convent was less than two hundred yards away, on the south side of Anlaby Road, from Tolkien's Medical Board. Supposing the writer did attend the boards in person, did he notice the Catholic establishment as he walked the pavements of Hull? Almost certainly, for the convent was a tall and imposing building, but what is not open to speculation, is that one of the nuns, Sister Mary Michael, visited Tolkien at Brooklands and became a lifelong friend. Unfortunately, the Anlaby Road Convent was completely destroyed during the air raids on Hull during the night of May 7th / 8th 1941. The site is now occupied by an electricity sub-station next to a block of flats.

Sister Mary Michael was based at Endsleigh House, a large mansion on Beverley Road, Hull. It had been purchased by the Sisters in 1901, as the convent on Anlaby Road had become overcrowded, and more room was needed for the community and the growing number of students. The location is ideal for visiting Brooklands Hospital, for it is only about three quarters of a mile to the west. Not only did Sister Mary remain a friend, but she also became godmother to Tolkien's second son, Michael, when he was born on October 22nd 1920. She stayed in touch with JRRT all her life, as evidenced by a letter written on March 11th 1949 (11) in which he describes her as a dear old friend. Mother Mary Michael was by that time an elderly lady about to celebrate her diamond jubilee – sixty years as a nun.

By then Sister Mary Michael was Mother Mary Michael. Endsleigh was also a training college, and one of the students, now called Sister Agnes, remembered meeting her in 1947. Apparently Mother Mary Michael was only short, but very formidable even in her final years. She was born as Mary McLaughlin in 1866, and entered the Convent at Anlaby Road in Hull in 1885, with her first profession being made on March 15th 1889 (12). In later life she lived in a Sisters of Mercy residential home at

Whitby, where Tolkien visited her on September 11th 1945. She died in Whitby on March 4th 1951.

So ends Hull's connection with Tolkien during the Great War. We now retrace the journey chronologically, and travel east to the pleasant Holderness seaside town of Hornsea, the author's first posting in the East Riding of Yorkshire in April 1917. If Hull is off the beaten track, then Holderness, the region east of the River Hull, is even more so. At the time of the Great War, it had regular railway services on the two branch lines to Hornsea and Withernsea, with reasonable road access to both towns. However, most other lanes were more fitted to the age of the horse drawn cart than the automobile.

Site of 130 Anlaby Road, looking east, the house was on the left hand side of the road, opposite the approaching white van. The photograph was taken from the front of the site of Anlaby Road Convent.

Did Tolkien notice this imposing Convent of the Sisters of Mercy on the south side of Anlaby Road when he had his medical examinations nearby on the north side? (Image courtesy of the Diocese of Middlesbrough)

Tolkien's medical report for September 4th 1918, when he was at Brooklands Military Hospital. (Courtesy of the National Archives, Kew)

Brooklands Military Hospital as it is today, the Dennison Centre opposite Hull University.

Endsleigh College, Hull in 2011. The Sisters of Mercy Convent where Sister Mary Michael was based in 1917.

Sister Mary Michael of Hull. The picture was probably taken on the occasion of her Diamond Jubilee as a nun in March 1949. (Image courtesy of the Institute of Our Lady of Mercy Archives, London)

Hornsea Rifle Range opening 1907. The article is taken from the Hull & East Riding Graphic Newspaper May 30th 1907 (Image courtesy of Hull History Centre)

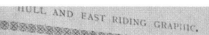

OPENING OF NEW RIFLE RANGE

HORNSEA.—Special for the GRAPHIC.

Mayor of Hull accompanied by Capt. Easton and Party proceeding to the New Range for the Opening Ceremony.

DESPITE the wretched climatic conditions on Thursday last, May 23rd, the opening of the new range at Hornsea, which all riflemen had been anxiously looking forward to, was a red-letter day in the history of the Hull Rifle Volunteer Corps. Over three hundred invitations had been issued, the guests including members of the Hull Corporation and donors who had given over £1,000 towards the range. The bad weather had evidently kept a lot away, but it was pleasing to note that a fair number of ladies attended.

The first part of the proceedings consisted of a party, with Colonel Jackson acting as guide, inspecting the range and its equipments. Splendid arrangements have been made for signalling and marking, and great interest was taken in the facilities offered for firing.

Amongst those present in addition to Colonel Jackson, V.D., were the Mayor, and Mayoress of Hull (Ald. and Mrs. Feldman), the Sheriff of Hull (Mr. J. J. T. Ferens) and Mrs. Ferens, Colonel Hammond, (Brigadier), Major Grant (Brigade Major), Major and Mrs. Haworth-Booth, Officers of the

Hull Artillery and Hull Rifle Volunteer Corps, and many others. Amongst the ladies present were Mrs. Jackson, the Misses Jackson, Mrs. Hall, Mrs. Scaam, Mrs. Shaw, Mrs. Thedman, Mrs. A. Simoam, Mrs. A. Easton, Miss Earle, and Miss Bolton.

After a few introductory remarks by Colonel Jackson, dwelling upon the advantages of the range, he called upon the Mayoress to fire the first shot on the range. The Bugler having sounded the commence firing, great cheering greeted the announcement by the marker that a bull's-eye had been recorded.

In proposing a vote of thanks to the Mayoress, Colonel Hammond paid a warm tribute to the Hull Corporation for their assistance in regard to the range. He hoped other places would follow their example.

Colonel Milburn, V.D., seconded. He hoped that favours would shortly come to the Artillery, and also to the Imperial Yeomanry.

Rousing cheers were given for the Mayoress.

The Mayor of Hull then responded to the vote of thanks accorded to the Mayoress. Whilst referring to the history of the volunteer movement, he felt sure that the volunteers and regulars would, when called upon, be ready to assist in the defence of their country.

Colonel Hall moved a vote of thanks to the donors, remarking that he thought the Corps had received full value for their money. (hear, hear.)

Mayor of Hull replying to a vote of thanks accorded the Mayoress for Opening the New Range, Hornsea, 23rd May, 1907.

In seconding, Colonel Shaw expressed the Corps' indebtedness to all those who had subscribed, and hoped that citizens would recognise they were entitled to assistance. The prize list was diminishing year by year, and more help would be greatly appreciated.

Major Judge responded, saying that this was the fourth range he had seen opened.

Mr. Bromby, in responding for the Hull Patriotic Rifle Club, said how deeply they were indebted to Colonel Jackson and the Officers of the Corps. (hear, hear). But for their kindness, they would most assuredly have had to cease to exist.

The formal proceedings having closed, tea was served to the guests, and the Battalion Band, under the able conductorship of Bandmaster Evans, played selections of music.

During the afternoon a shooting match took place between volunteer teams (two sides) captained by Colonel Snow and Major Scaam, resulting in a win for Major Scaam's team, by 27 points.

The First Competition on the New Range at Hornsea, May 23rd, 1907.

Hornsea

For a small Yorkshire resort, Hornsea had the good fortune to possess not one, but two North Eastern Railway stations – Hornsea Bridge, which is half a mile before what later became known as Hornsea (Town) station. It is the first station that is of interest, for in the immediate vicinity is Bank Terrace. It is number 1 Bank Terrace that concerns us, for when Tolkien was sent to the Yorkshire coast, Edith and cousin Jennie Grove followed him and took up lodgings there. The station would have loomed above the house, on an embankment, and Edith would have only to walk down the sloping path and round the corner to find herself on Bank Terrace. She was probably confident that having gained accommodation in the town, she would be close to her husband, who had been assigned to the 3rd Lancashire Fusiliers' outpost and musketry school at Hornsea. Her choice of a lodging place was excellent, for the musketry camp was less than a mile south along Rolston Road, the main Withernsea road that runs past the end of Bank Terrace, so it was just a pleasant walk away. However, almost immediately after she had taken up residence, Tolkien was sent further south in the county, to Thirtle Bridge, near Withernsea. His departure started a steady flow of correspondence between them. From May 5th 1917, (13) letters and envelopes exist that show her writing to him at Thirtle Bridge from 1 Bank Terrace, Hornsea, although one letter, and a postcard dated May 12th, did get redirected back to the musketry school at Hornsea. Having paid the rent, she dutifully stayed at 1 Bank Terrace until June 1st. I believe that she must have paid in advance until the end of the month, and then attempted to obtain lodgings nearer to her husband at Thirtle Bridge. What is certain, is that June 1st was the last date of correspondence from Edith at this address. What is not so certain, is where she lodged for the next six weeks, but I will look at this matter later. At the time, Edith would have rented her accommodation from the Shepherd family who owned the property, for the 1915 Electoral Register has Richard Henry Shepherd there, and the 1918 one has a certain George Ernest Shepherd and his wife, Sallie, residing with him in the house. The Kelly's Local Directory of 1913 also records the presence of George Ernest Shepherd at 1 Bank Terrace.

Our next port of call in Hornsea is the musketry camp used for rifle training. The 1916 Lancashire Fusiliers Annual records that (14) Sergeant J Grimshaw, V.C., a hero of the 'Lancashire Landing', was the musketry instructor to the recruits there. Wherever it was, Tolkien did not spend long there, for he was posted there on April 19th 1917 (15), but within days his name is associated with Thirtle Bridge. He may even have been dispatched on arrival straight on to Thirtle Bridge. However, the address crops up on an envelope dated May 5th, a postcard dated May 12th and rather oddly, another letter, dated July 14th

(16). The first two envelopes had been re-directed to the musketry camp, but the last one was re-directed from the camp! All three communications were from his wife, Edith. It is therefore probable that the author did spend a little time at Hornsea Musketry Camp. The only published picture of Tolkien at this time is reproduced on page 41 of The Tolkien Family Album, John & Priscilla Tolkien, HarperCollins, 1992. It shows a very slender and gaunt Ronald, with Edith at his side, on the beach at Hornsea, and is dated 1917. The military obviously believed he was billeted there, otherwise they would not have re-directed his post from Thirtle Bridge on two occasions. Furthermore, despite the country being at war, I am confident that Edith would have had a reasonable idea where her husband was. She would not have written from Withernsea on July 14th to the musketry camp, if she believed her husband to be only three miles down the road north at Thirtle Bridge.

The military records are vague on the exact location of the musketry camp at Hornsea, but there is one location that fits the bill perfectly – the site that is known locally as Rolston Camp. I had been aware for many years of a field about a mile south of Hornsea that housed a number of timber huts that looked to be of military origin. The last few remaining were only demolished during the present century. The site now has some luxury lodges on, and in a field to the south of them is a forlorn concrete building of unknown purpose. The range must have been nearly three quarters of a mile long from north to south. Subsequent research has shown that a rifle range, funded by donors including the Hull Corporation, opened on the site on May 23rd 1907 (17). It was for the use of the Hull Rifle Volunteer Corps, and on the opening day there was a competition between them, and the Officers of the Hull Artillery. After the war, in 1921, it became an army camp. It is easy to understand why the 3rd Lancashire Fusiliers would choose to occupy it in the event of war, and use it for coastal defence. It retained a rifle training function, as a number of soldiers attended courses there during the 1st World War. The camp has had a number of owners over the years. In the 1930s, it was the Hull Boys' Club, before being sold to Hull Corporation in 1939. It came into the possession of Humberside County Council when the authority was formed in 1974, but reverted back to Hull City Council in 1989, when it was used by schools and youth groups from Humberside and the West Riding of Yorkshire. Part of the site had been sold, but in December 2010, the Jubilee Holiday fund, which is administered by the Hull City Council, put the remainder of the site up for sale, as it had not been used since 1992 because of the need for repairs (18).

Our final stopping off point in Hornsea is 'Waverley', Cliff Road. There is just one reference to the house in the addresses on correspondence between JRRT and Edith, and it is dated July 14th 1917. Edith, now at Withernsea, had sent a letter to her husband addressed to the musketry camp, but it was re-addressed to 'Waverley', Cliff Road, Hornsea (19). Tolkien was due to take a signalling examination, which he subsequently failed, at Dunstable in July 1917. He was there from approximately July 20th to July 25th, and so was away from his home base, which at the time would have been Thirtle Bridge. I think it possible that before travelling down to Dunstable, he passed through his initial 3rd Lancashire Fusilier placing, Hornsea Musketry Camp. Unfortunately, it appears that they may have had no accommodation at the camp and so used temporary digs for Tolkien. Furthermore, Cliff Road would have been more convenient for catching the train south at Hornsea station than either Thirtle Bridge or Rolston Camp. The property belonged to John Wardale, sometimes spelt Wardle, whose occupation was described as insurance agent in the 1911 Census. He is listed as the owner in the 1913 and 1921 Kelly's Directory, and also as a freehold owner in the 1915 Electoral Register. It would appear at first glance that locating a house with an address would be very easy indeed. Nothing could be further from the truth! In 2012, there is no house called 'Waverley' on Cliff Road. What had happened over the last century was that 'Waverley', owned by Charles Crowther Hart in 1901 according to the Kelly's Local Directory of the same year, had by 1905 become 9 Clifton Terrace. The saga did not end there though, for Clifton Terrace no longer exists either! By tracking the Electoral Registers right through the 20th century, I discovered that between 1946 and 1947, addresses were simplified after the 2nd World War, and 9 Clifton Terrace, Cliff Road finally became just 79 Cliff Road!

We now travel roughly twelve miles south down the Holderness coast, to a village that has a special place in the minds of all Tolkien fans – Roos.

1 Bank Terrace, Hornsea. Edith's first lodgings in East Yorkshire when she arrived in 1917.

Rolston Camp Lodges, looking south. This is how the site of Hornsea Musketry Camp looked in 2011.

79 Cliff Road, Hornsea. Tolkien had a short stay here in July 1917, while travelling to, or from, Dunstable for a signalling examination.

Postcard c1900 of Dent's Garth, with the Sunday School, long since gone, on the left.

Roos

Roos is the location where Tolkien reality merges with myth. The place name is quoted so often in the literature about JRRT, that I believe that this sleepy Holderness village has acquired a mystique all of its own. Unfortunately, there is little in the way of hard facts to support the many rumours about this rural idyll.

The focal point for Tolkien fans centres on Edith dancing for her husband in 'a small woodland glade filled with hemlocks at Roos in Yorkshire'. Nowhere does the story-teller state precisely where this sylvan retreat was to be found. Following John Garth in 'Tolkien and the Great War' all commentators, including me, agree that the wooded glade was Dents Garth, at the very southern edge of the village. After the death of Edith in 1971, Tolkien recalled in a letter to his son Christopher, how his wife had enchanted him by dancing and singing in a small copse at Roos (20). Tolkien claimed that this magical spectacle in the heart of an English shire inspired the 'Tale of Luthien Tinuviel and Beren', and he considered that this event formed the centrepiece of what would become 'The Silmarillion'. I believe that the identity of Dents Garth is correct for several reasons. To begin with, Tolkien was stationed only a mile and a half away at Thirtle Bridge. We are not sure if Edith was lodged with him, or whether she was in hired quarters locally, but we do know that she was in the early stages of pregnancy. Dents

Garth is only a gentle stroll from the centre of Roos village, and if one approaches the wood from the direction of the church, they would both have been suddenly surprised by the grand vista of Holderness that would unfold before them. Nothing on the Main Street of Roos, where the traffic now drives continually through to Hornsea and Withernsea, can prepare you for the totally different aspect that this corner of the county presents to you. Also, I am certain that Tolkien would have been drawn to All Saints' Church, for it is a gem, and has a novel feature. Not only is the approach up the steps and through an avenue of yew trees delightful, but this place of worship has a watchtower on the north side! Originally dating from Norman times (21), by the 20th century the watchtower was much diminished in size, but it is an oddity none the less that would surely have appealed to the eccentric in Tolkien's nature.

As to the date when this scene was enacted, Humphrey Carpenter in his biography of 1977 states that the event took place in early 1918, but this is clearly incorrect, for Tolkien was then at Easington, over 12 miles away, and it is unknown if his wife was still in the area. Furthermore, she had had a difficult time with the birth of their first child, John Frances Reuel, and would certainly have not felt like dancing. Additionally, no one finds hemlock flowering in winter. The balance of the evidence suggests that Edith danced in May or June 1917, when the plant was in bloom and the days light, and the weather was very fair. How do we know this? Because an intelligence report, dated July 26th 1917, of the East Yorkshire Regiment camped at Withernsea, concludes with the following snippet 'The weather since April has been of an exceptional nature, brilliantly fine and warm' (22). That is, ideal weather for joyous dancing in a sun dappled copse. All available evidence points to Edith's dance being at Dents Garth in the late spring of 1917.

There is another spot locally that is rumoured to have influenced JRRT's writing, and that is a piece of land known locally as 'The Bog'. It is situated just over a mile south west of the village, down a farm track. The location is certainly unusual, and will have changed little since Tolkien's time, being several acres of trees, apparently growing out of water that has collected in a deep depression in the rolling fields. Holderness is often described as being flat, but any visitor who takes the time to ramble around the area will discover that this is not the case. Those of an imaginative disposition believe that 'The Bog' could have inspired 'The Dead Marshes' in Lord of the Rings, but I am not very convinced, as he is much more likely to have been influenced, and more profoundly, by his experiences in the trenches.

We now come to a more contentious issue – did JRRT or Edith take up residence in the village during his posting to Yorkshire? If they did, I have to say that there is no local evidence to support this claim, only rumours. All that Tolkien himself mentions is 'a lonely house near Roos' in his correspondence (23). Surely if he were lodged in Roos, he would not call it 'near Roos'. Furthermore, he was stationed at Thirtle Bridge, which is near Roos, and is indeed a very lonely location. He had no need to billet in the village, and indeed, as an officer in the 3rd Lancashire Fusiliers, he would surely be required to be on the base. As to whether his wife took up rooms at Roos, as has been suggested, it is possible. However, on balance, I feel it is more likely that she managed to stay with JRRT at the camp. Edith must have left 1 Bank Terrace, Hornsea on June 1st 1917. There is no communication extant that covers the period up to July 12th, when she sent a letter to JRRT from Withernsea. Where was she between those dates? The lack of any correspondence could mean that it has been lost with the passage of time, but it looks almost certain that Edith did manage to share residence with her husband for those missing six weeks. In 1972, commenting on the conception of the 'Tale of Tinuviel', JRRT remembered his 'brief time in command of an outpost of the Humber Garrison in 1917, and she (Edith) was able to live with me for a while' (24). It was obviously only of a temporary arrangement, otherwise Edith would not have moved on to Withernsea in July. Therefore, is it possible that she stayed at the officers' quarters for the Humber Garrison at Tunstall Hall? Unlikely, for surely the other officers would want a similar privilege, although as a commanding officer,

JRRT may have had preference. This would raise another question, what became of cousin Jennie Grove, who had been at Hornsea - she surely couldn't have lodged with them at Tunstall Hall! Maybe they all did manage to rent accommodation in Roos so that they could be together, but where that could have been is open to speculation. What is certain, is that there were women at Thirtle Bridge Camp. Concerts were organised, and the Countess of Westmorland, wife of the Commanding Officer of the battalion, and her maid, Miss A.D. Farrington, appeared in several of the plays and sketches in 1917 and 1918. Additionally, Mrs R.W. Stocks, the wife of the Medical Officer was also involved (25). Therefore, as at least two of the officers had spouses there, it is not unreasonable to assume that Tolkien may have been afforded a similar privilege, albeit for a limited period. Of course, it is possible that all the ladies lodged locally, and visited the camp for the theatrical productions. However, JRRT, in stating that Edith was 'able to live with me for a while', surely indicates that in all probability, she was able to share accommodation at the camp.

Putting that aside, looking at the rumours that surround the author and his wife's possible lodgings in Roos, we are presented with three possible dwellings. Firstly, hearsay identifies what is now the Old Rectory as Tolkien's lodging place. It was built between 1892 and 1893, and the incumbent, who arrived in 1891 and was there until 1921, was one Reverend

Edward Milsom (26). The house is certainly large, but whether the good vicar ever entertained lodgers one can only guess. It is certainly a very pleasant stroll from here along Rectory Lane to All Saints' Church and Dents Garth. The next candidate for speculation is 'the house next to the post office'. Again, this statement would seem to make it clear where this house is located in the village. Unfortunately, this is not the case, for in 1917, the post office was not situated where the current one is. In the early part of the 20th century, the post office was on the north corner of Hodgson Lane, adjacent to Coltman Row, sometimes spelt Coultman Row. This is a hundred yards south, and on the opposite side of the main street, to the current establishment. So 'the house next to the post office' presents us with several possibilities, either side of two sites. I have included images of both locations, but I would not give too much credence to either. The tradition appears to date back to around 1968, when a local schoolboy, for a project, wrote about the Tolkien connection with the village (27). It is possible that a pupil might have talked to older residents of the village, but it is questionable whether they would remember one particular individual out of the thousands of military personnel that passed through Holderness in the Great War. I will leave it to the reader to decide whether a pupil at school in the 1960s had access to knowledge that has since been lost. It is possible, but not probable.

Dent's Garth House, Roos, in 2010, looking west toward the wood.

Roos All Saints' Church in 2010, with Dent's Garth Wood at the back.

Roos All Saints' Church in 2010, highlighting its unusual feature, the watchtower.

The Bog at Roos in 2011. It will not have changed much since Tolkien's stay in the area in 1917 – Holderness at its remote and rural best.

One possible residence for JRRT and Edith in Roos in 1917 was the Old Rectory, which at the time was a quite new rectory, having being built around 1893.

Another possible lodging place for the Tolkiens was beside the old Roos post office, which was the building on the right of the road junction in 1917.

Or did the Tolkiens stay beside the current post office at Roos?

War Office Letter, confirming Tolkien's arrival at Thirtle Bridge, and noting the Lancashire Fusiliers H.Q. as Tunstall Hall. (Courtesy of the National Archives, Kew)

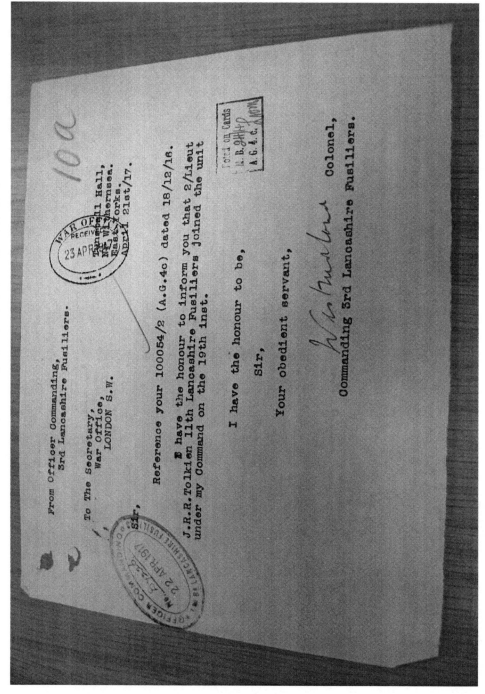

From Officer Commanding,
3rd Lancashire Fusiliers.

To The Secretary,
War Office,
LONDON S.W.

Thirtle Hall,
Nr. Withernsea.
East Yorks.
April 21st/17.

10a

WAR OFFICE
RECEIVED
23 APR

Sir,

Reference your 100054/2 (A.G.4c) dated 18/12/16.

I have the honour to inform you that 2/Lieut
J.R.R.Tolkien 11th Lancashire Fusiliers joined the unit
under my Command on the 19th inst.

I have the honour to be,

Sir,

Your obedient servant,

Colonel,
Commanding 3rd Lancashire Fusiliers.

Thirtle Bridge, Tunstall and Withernsea

I have devoted one chapter to these three places because it is almost impossible to disentangle Tolkien's stay with the 3rd Lancashire Fusiliers at Thirtle Bridge Camp from the other two localities. Confusingly, in some of the War Office records, the camp is sometimes misspelt as 'Thirkle Bridge' or 'Thirtley Bridge' (and in 'The Shaping of Middle-earth', volume 4 of Christopher Tolkien's History of Middle-earth, it is miscalled 'Thistle Bridge').

A letter of April 21st 1917 (28) from the Commanding Officer, Colonel Westmorland, based at the Tunstall Hall, to the War Office, confirms that JRRT had joined the 3rd Lancashire Fusiliers, a reserve battalion, on April 19th. Interestingly, the letter also alludes to correspondence on December 18th 1916, which confirms that they had been expecting Tolkien in Holderness for several months. Incidentally, Tunstall Hall was the third H.Q. for the 3rd Reserve Battalion of the Lancashire Fusiliers in the area, having started at Sutton-on-Hull, and then Ottringham (see first chapter). By some strange coincidence, April 19th (29) was also the precise date that three companies, A, B and D, of the 3rd East Yorkshire Regiment moved from hired quarters elsewhere in Holderness to a field next to Osgerby's Laundry, where the works was located on South Cliff. This is clearly at the south end of the town, and known locally, for obvious reasons, as the Laundry Field. It must have been a time of considerable change, for there was further activity at Thirtle Bridge the following day, when recruits in the regiment moved from their base at Sutton-on-Hull to a canvas camp at Thirtle Bridge (30).

Tolkien's first stay at Thirtle Bridge was to last until mid-August 1917, when he had a recurrence of trench fever and ended up in Brooklands Hospital, Hull, about the 13th of the month. Although his promotion to full lieutenant was not effected until November 24th 1917, this promotion was backdated to July 1st, when he was at the camp (31). He held ambitions of being a signals officer at the camp, but surprisingly, the same month he failed the test at Dunstable. This must surely have been due to his ill health, for one cannot imagine a man of his considerable linguistic abilities not otherwise being successful. His second turn of duty came after he came back from Brooklands Hospital in Hull on October 16th 1917 (32). Tolkien was then at the camp for a month, when another medical board sat on November 16th and recommended that he continue his turn of duty at Thirtle Bridge. Strangely, in the light of this recommendation, he subsequently moved south to Easington instead (more of this report in the next chapter). The final stint at Thirtle Bridge was from March 19th 1918, when he was examined once more by the medical board at the Humber Garrison. He then returned to Thirtle Bridge until another board sat on April 10th, when he was re-examined. This report stated 'He has recovered', and rated his disability at nil, finding him fit for general service and instructing him to continue with the 3rd Lancs. Fus. at Thirtle Bridge until further orders (33). Despite this instruction, he was sent back to his home territory in the Midlands, first at Penkridge Camp, Rugeley, and then on to nearby Brocton Camp, Cannock Chase.

There is an extant letter from Edith (34), dated July 10th 1918, that is addressed to her husband at Thirtle Bridge, but this is surely a mistake, as he was by then back in Brooklands Hospital, Hull, after contracting gastritis at Brocton Camp, Staffordshire on June 29th. There is no evidence that Tolkien returned to Thirtle Bridge after he left in April 1918.

The camp was based at a bend three miles north west of Withernsea on what is now designated the B1242 road to Hornsea, at a point where it passes over Tunstall Drain. It existed to train new recruits for the front and to guard against any assault from the sea. The base was initially a tented one, set up in 1916, but by the time that the writer arrived, the site was covered with wooden hutments, and at least four brick buildings, one of which was the officers' mess. The 1910 Ordnance Survey map shows no buildings at the site, and so the brick buildings may well have been purpose built for the army. Three of the brick structures have long been demolished, but they appear to have included a wash house and a gate house. The third building's use is unknown. However, the officers' mess still exists, close to the road, and is now called Mona House. Only the most western part of the building, nearest the road, is of First World War origin. The dwelling has naturally been much modernised and extended, but the residents are fully aware of the building's historic links with the great author. Stewart Hodgson is the current resident in the historic front portion, and he has kindly allowed me to reproduce his plan of the site as it was in the 1950s. Elaine Dunn, his mother-in-law, lives in the rear part of Mona House. How the dwelling came to acquire the name is unknown. On a military establishment, it is unlikely to refer to a girl's name, though it might be some obscure army acronym that includes 'officers' in it. Another possibility is that it is named after the Battle of Mona on April 19th 1782, during the American Revolutionary War (35). Britain was victorious over France when they fought for control over the Mona Passage between Puerto Rico and Hispaniola in the Caribbean. There is some precedent for the naming after a battle like this, as A Company, Humberside & South Yorkshire Army Cadet Force, are housed at Mona House, Sutton-on-Hull, which, as mentioned earlier, had been a base for recruits in the Lancashire Fusiliers during 1916. Fortunately, the bungalow has been owned by the same family for many decades, which has permitted some vestige of local memories of the camp to survive into the 21st century. However, it is only a very small awareness, for most folk in East Yorkshire, even in the immediate vicinity, do not know of the existence of a World War 1 army camp that housed nearly 1,500 soldiers and about 60 officers at any one time. In fact, over 15,000 men, and nearly 700 officers were sent out from the camp during its short existence. The site was cleared immediately after the Great War, and any buildings and building materials were auctioned off on August 11th 1919 by N Easton and Sons, Bowlalley Lane, Hull, on the instructions of the Surplus Government Disposal Board, Ministry of Munitions (36). This left the land largely unchanged until mid-century when it came into the possession of the Hodgsons. A drainage system covers the site, connecting what would have been the wooden and brick huts, which may have included the officers' living quarters, to presumably a cess-pit in the vicinity. One other World War 1 building also survives – the cookhouse. It is a wooden structure, now plated with corrugated iron and used as a barn, about a hundred yards back from the road, east of Mona House. Entry to the camp was via a rough farm track, known locally as the Camp Road, also just to the east of Mona House. The land on which Thirtle Bridge Camp resided is now farmed by Stuart Smales of Renish Farm, just to the south of Thirtle Bridge.

About half the officers at the camp were unfit, and at Thirtle Bridge Tolkien met at least two old acquaintances from his former regiment, the 11th Lancashire Fusiliers (37). One was

Fawcett-Barry, who was adjutant there. He had formerly been the commander of 'A' Company. Also present was Lieutenant-Colonel Bird, who had been Tolkien's commanding officer on the Somme. At Thirtle Bridge, he was classified as being a major according to the Lancashire Fusiliers Annual, and was involved at the camp with events such as sports, concerts and plays. Nearby at the H.Q. at Tunstall Hall, which was also officers' quarters, JRRT's pal Leslie Risdon Huxtable was recovering, having been buried alive in the trenches on October 10th the previous year. At this juncture, I will now introduce two other characters who have helped to add to our knowledge of Thirtle Bridge.

The first is Captain Gilbert Mackereth, who had signed up, by strange coincidence, at Oxford, Tolkien's university town, in July 1916 (38). He was a Manchester man, serving with the 17th Battalion Lancashire Fusiliers. After being injured, he came back to Britain, and upon completion of three weeks sick leave, he joined Colonel Westmorland at Thirtle Bridge on March 16th 1918. Soon after March 19th, Tolkien arrived back at the camp for his third turn of duty there, before being dispatched south on April 10th for Penkridge Camp. Mackereth was sent back overseas on June 10th 1918 (39). It is possible, indeed even probable that the two men became acquainted in those three weeks – all the more so because Tolkien had been friends with John Mackreth at Exeter College, Oxford, and would doubtless have been struck by the similarity of their names (SOURCE NOTE: John Garth, 'Tolkien, Exeter College and the Great War', in Tolkien's The Lord of the Rings: Sources of Inspiration, ed. Stratford Caldecott and Thomas Honegger [Zurich: Walking Tree, 2008]), but what is significant from an historical point of view is that thanks to Mackereth, a photograph of Thirtle Bridge Camp has survived into the present century!

The other man who adds to the Thirtle Bridge story is Owen Ashton, from Llawryglyn, who joined up in 1916. His rank is not known, but some of his letters have survived in the Powys County Archives Office (40), and he appears to have served at some time with the 3rd Lancashire Fusiliers. Ashton probably arrived at the camp in February 1917, and after short stays elsewhere, he was there until at least May 27th. He did not think much of the place, and said so in some of his letters. What is interesting though, for Tolkien afficionados, is that he was censured by the authorities for writing many of his early letters in Welsh. It is even possible that Tolkien was charged with the act of censorship, for this was one of the unpopular and divisive duties required of officers. Geoffrey Bache Smith, one of the members of the Tea Club and Barrovian Society, who had been killed on the Somme in December 1916, left some books on Welsh, including the Mabinogion (the Welsh cycle of legends), to Tolkien (41). At the time, the writer was developing words and etymologies for his own Welsh-influenced language, which he called Gnomish or Goldogrin. The dictionary of this new language was deemed by Tolkien to have been the creation of Eriol, and its Gnomish title was i-Lam na-Ngoldathon. The document that records this, also has the note in Gnomish 'Tol Withernon (and places besides), 1917. This is surely a reference to nearby Withernsea. Tol in the writer's created language means island, which, as John Garth has argued, may show a recognition by Tolkien that the sea shaped and defined the locality. One can speculate whether JRRT met Owen Ashton. Did he enjoy the company of a fluent Welsh speaker – just at the time that he was devising his own Welsh inspired tongue? I believe that it is probable that the two men did meet, for duties at the camp, as described in letters home, were tedious, and boredom was rife. Ashton and Tolkien were both at the camp for several weeks, and I am sure that the author would have used his time well, and made the most of any resource that would assist in developing his mythology. He was fit, but not fighting fit; he couldn't return home, or access a university library, but he could make the most of the opportunities presented to him, possibly in the form of the Welshman Owen Ashton. Incidentally, like Tolkien, Ashton had passed through Hornsea Musketry Camp during his military career.

Having mentioned Tolkien's creation of the Welsh-based Gnomish while at Thirtle Bridge, I will examine other aspects of his writing that were taking form in the spring and summer of 1917. He had been working on a poem called 'Sea Chant of an Elder Day' for a while and he developed it further at this time, ultimately renaming it 'The Horns of Ulmo' later in 1917. A surviving manuscript, originally written in March 1915, includes an addition, probably written about this time, of a prose introduction that connects the poem to the fall of Gondolin, becoming 'the song that Tuor told to Earendel'. During all this period, Tolkien's imagined world was taking form.

It is due to John Garth's extensive research that we are now aware of the influence that Holderness had on Tolkien's writing. There are a number of reasons why this should be the case. Although Tolkien was born in Bloemfontein, Orange Free State in 1892, he was brought up in urban England, among the conurbations and heavily industrialised areas around Birmingham and the West Midlands. Even today, and more particularly in the early 20th century, Holderness was a complete contrast. It was a land of broad acres of gently rolling fields, isolated hamlets, and scattered small villages with little in the way of road access, most of which were not metalled until after the war. Added to that was the sea – the North Sea, which had incidentally, prior to the Great War, been called the German Ocean. Tolkien was a citizen of middle England, literally, for coastline of any description was at least a hundred miles away from where he grew up. Yet the sea influenced his writing considerably, especially - as John Garth argues in 'Tolkien and the Great War' - the one that was gnawing away inexorably at the fabric of his beloved England at the rate of two yards every single year. The coast of Holderness had lost nearly thirty towns to these insatiable waters since the Norman invasion. The camp at Thirtle Bridge was close to several – Monkwike, Sand-le-Mere, Waxholme, and Owthorne. As a lover of history, he would surely have heard tales of the once famous town of Ravenser, mentioned in Shakespeare. It grew as a major port in the region of Spurn Point in the 13th century, and was then overwhelmed by the waves in the 14th century. This is a coastline where the relentless sea becomes gradually embedded in the psyche, a point of reference to anyone who dwells for long in Holderness. Indeed, the sea was a provider, for the East Coast was well known for its fishing, but in Holderness it also took away, devouring villages, scattering their shattered remnants on the shore, forcing the inhabitants inland and on the defensive. The gradual attacks by the sea and the loss of entire villages would have fed the imagination of the man, who, in the 1930s, wrote the Atlantis-inspired tale of the Downfall of Nýmenor.

As an academic, he was critical of the way that the Norman culture had subsumed the native language and tales of England. Interestingly, he found himself in a corner of the land where that influence had been felt less severely. After the Conquest in 1066, William ordered that the north be laid waste, and to this end he sent his armies forth. However, upon reaching Beverley, the officer in charge fell from his horse and broke his neck in such a manner that his head faced backwards. The king, being superstitious, believed this to be a warning from St. John of Beverley, and the hordes rode north, leaving the territories of St. John, most of Holderness, unmolested (42). Tolkien, as a lover of and expert on language, may have realised that many words in the area still had echoes of Anglo-Saxon in them. Indeed, words that had long fallen out of use elsewhere, survived in Holderness until recent times. Added to this, it is worth noting that Tolkien resided in Leeds in the 1920s, and that he took a keen interest in the local dialect. It is understood that he became a member of the Yorkshire Dialect Society, and even added a preface to Walter E Haigh's 1928 volume 'New Glossary of the Dialect of the Huddersfield District' (43).

I am confident that not only did Holderness give him inspiration, but it also gave him time to reflect and write. He may have written while in France, but camp life at the front, and in appalling conditions, was surely not conducive to mental concentration. Tolkien himself observed that scribbling on bits of paper and envelopes while crouched in filth made serious creativity nigh impossible (44). Nearly all the War Office records show that while JRRT was in East Yorkshire, he was a man unfit to return to active service. Surely his duties therefore, would generally have been light, and the hours probably weighed heavily on him as he looked out across the North Sea, scanning the horizon for an invasion that fortunately never arrived. The camp was placed away from towns and villages, surrounded by open fields, and it would have been relatively easy for Tolkien to find solitude and space for his imagination to function. This brings us neatly to the next place on our tour – Tunstall.

The village of Tunstall is just over a mile north of Thirtle Bridge, but Tunstall Hall is somewhat nearer. As I have recorded elsewhere, this was not only the H.Q. of the Humber Garrison of the 3rd Lancashire Fusiliers, but apparently also officers' quarters (45), and Tolkien would certainly have visited Huxtable there. Both Tolkien and Huxtable attended a Minden Day meal on August 1st 1917, and it was not long after this that the author succumbed once more to the trench fever. Huxtable was not to be at Tunstall much longer either, for he was to return to France on September 8th (46). The meal was an annual regimental occasion, and purely for the 3rd Battalion Lancashire Fusiliers. Tolkien had his menu card signed by over twenty other fellow officers (47), but unfortunately there is no indication where the event took place. I believe it is almost certain that the meal took place at the Regimental Institute at Thirtle Bridge. The Lancashire Fusilier Annuals record that the institute was 'well equipped, with a stage' (48). Furthermore, in April 1917, the institute was provided with electric lighting. The size of the place can be judged from the rebuild and alterations that took place in May 1918, (49) enabling it to accommodate no less than 850 people! What would have been more natural than to seat all the attendants at the meal in such an adequate hall on the camp? Moreover, following a suggestion in 1916 by Captain Temple-Powell and Major Blencowe, a proscenium had been designed by Major L.G. Bird and completed by Corporal Boyer. The design included the regimental crest draped with curtains of the regimental colour. There were scrolls bearing the battle-honours of the regiment on the left, and new honours, subject to amendment, were added on the right, so that Ypres, Lancashire Landing, Salonica and Somme figure in the design (50). Surely, this was the ideal location for such an important regimental event. Any other location looks unlikely - why travel, even to Withernsea, if such facilities were available close to hand? Even Tunstall Hall would probably have been inferior to the facilities readily available at the Regimental Institute.

We now move on to Tunstall beach, were there was a lookout post at the end of the Tunstall Drain to help defend the coast, at a location better know as Sand-le-Mere. We know that 'Z' Company moved from Holmpton to Sand-le-Mere on June 16th 1916, (51) with Thirtle Bridge Camp just a mile west of here, along the drain. Sand-le-Mere appears in Owen Ashton's writings, for on May 13th 1917, at a time when Tolkien was at Thirtle Bridge, he wrote to his parents, in Welsh, a letter from Zand sur Mere, near Withernsea, which can only mean this location. It sounds as if he wrote the missive while stationed in the lookout post there. I am confident that Tolkien would have also covered turns of duty at this spot. What he may well have noticed, in the context of his fascination with the merciless sea and the land vulnerable to its assault, was the submarine forest that lay on the sands within a few hundred yards of the outpost at the mouth of Tunstall Drain. The stumps located at Tunstall, near the present Sand-le-Mere caravan park, are often exposed, a constant reminder of the voracious appetite of these turbulent waters. The ghosts of lands departed were there before Tolkien's very eyes, waiting to be awoken, and woven into the fabric of his epic tales. I am of the opinion that the long hours on watch at this windswept spot would not have been wasted, and would have been creatively profitable ones for him. There is also another submarine forest at Withernsea, aptly named Noah's Wood, which is normally covered by sand and gravel, as the sea defences of the resort include groynes that enable it to accumulate.

I believe that Thirtle Bridge was chosen as a site for a camp because of its defensive potential in the eventuality of a German invasion. Holderness is a low lying region that rises gently towards the coast. The boulder clay cliffs are mostly high, varying between twenty feet and nearly one hundred feet ten miles further south at Dimlington. The cliffs are virtually non-existent at Kilnsea and Spurn, but these two locations had substantial batteries, with many troops and armaments to defend them. This was not the case at Tunstall, or more precisely Sand-le-Mere beach. It was an ideal site for an invasion, as ten foot high clay is hardly a barrier to any serious seaborne invasion. The only defensible feature along this stretch of coast is Tunstall Drain, for it is about ten feet deep, and at least as wide. Advancing foot soldiers would have been seriously inconvenienced by it. Therefore, whichever way the enemy troops had attempted to advance, the Humber Garrison would have situated themselves on the north or south bank of the drain as appropriate. In the likelihood of invasion, the seemingly purposeless deployment of men to defend a drainage ditch would have taken on strategic importance.

Withernsea is next on the agenda. It is seaside resort that came into being in its present form with the arrival of the railway in 1854. The population of what had once only been a collection of hamlets then rose dramatically and by the close of the Edwardian era, it was a very popular resort for visitors from Hull and the West Riding of Yorkshire. As mentioned earlier in the book, by 1917, many troops were already based in the immediate area.

Having left 1 Bank Terrace, Hornsea on June 1st of that year, Edith either stayed with her husband, probably at Thirtle Bridge, or possibly at Roos. What is known, is that by July 12th, she had lodgings at 76 Queen Street, Withernsea (52). The property was in the hands of the Bishop family, for the 1915 Electoral Register lists one Robert James Bishop as the owner. In the 1918 register it was just plain James Bishop. The 1913 and 1921 Kelly's Local Directory concurs, noting James Bishop as owner on both occasions. 72 Queen Street, Withernsea, also belonged to this gentleman, for Kelly's Directory records both houses as having apartments available to rent from him. The house has since been annexed by 78 Queen Street, which in the early 20th century housed the business of one J. Westerdale, but is now the Lifeboat Cafe. Thus, it is now possible to enjoy a meal while seated in the building that once had been the lodging place for Tolkien's wife! With her husband at Thirtle Bridge, just three miles away, Edith must have seen much of him, for there were frequent trips by pony and cart from the station (53), which was just a couple of hundred yards further south on Queen Street. Unfortunately, she was soon deprived of such convenience, as about August 13th Tolkien was admitted into Brooklands Officers Hospital, Cottingham Road, Hull. We know this, for Edith posted a letter on the 14th to JRRT at the hospital. Once again, she had moved to be close to her husband, and once more, fate had intervened. She had already been deprived of his company when he travelled down to Dunstable in the middle of July, writing not one, but two letters to him on July 14th; the first to Hornsea Musketry Camp, subsequently redirected to 'Waverley', Cliff Road, Hornsea, and the second one re-addressed to him at R.E. Signal Depot, Dunstable. I believe that it was due to his imminent departure for Dunstable, via Hornsea, that Edith had to find before July 14th, alternative lodgings to Thirtle Bridge Camp. With her husband in command at the camp, her stay may have been tolerated. With him 200 miles away taking an examination, her presence, unaccompanied, on a military camp was unlikely to have been acceptable. With Edith now in residence at 76 Queen Street, JRRT arrived back at Thirtle Bridge some time about the 25th. This was obviously a surprise to Edith, for she had sent a letter to him at Dunstable on the 21st, and it was re-directed all the way back to Withernsea! Edith wrote a number of letters to JRRT while she was lodged in Queen Street, with the last one dated August 21st, when she finally abandoned attempting to follow his movements in Yorkshire, and left the delights of the east coast and headed to 37 Montpellier Villas, Cheltenham (54). Whether she ever returned to the East Riding of Yorkshire during Tolkien's military service is a subject of considerable controversy, as we shall see later.

We now start the final leg of our journey around the Tolkien Triangle, heading even further south, and passing through Withernsea, to the quiet village of Easington, about seven miles away from the resort.

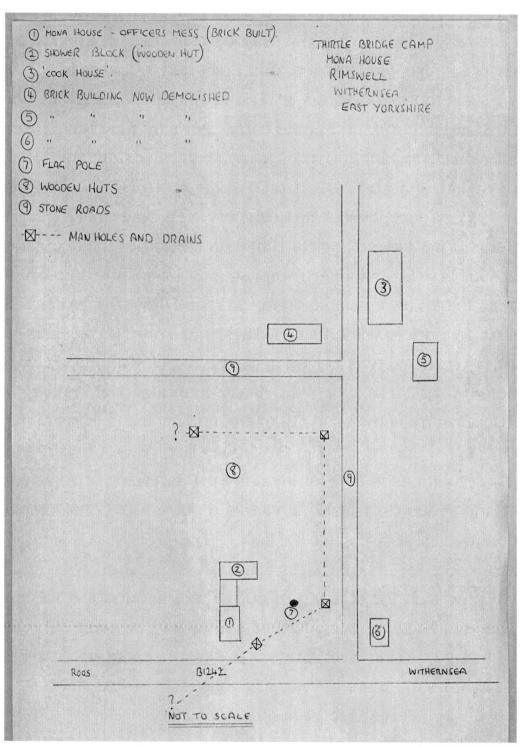

① 'MONA HOUSE' - OFFICERS MESS. (BRICK BUILT).
② SHOWER BLOCK (WOODEN HUT).
③ 'COOK HOUSE'.
④ BRICK BUILDING NOW DEMOLISHED
⑤ "   "   "   "
⑥ "   "   "   "
⑦ FLAG POLE
⑧ WOODEN HUTS
⑨ STONE ROADS
⊠--- MAN HOLES AND DRAINS

THIRTLE BRIDGE CAMP
MONA HOUSE
RIMSWELL
WITHERNSEA
EAST YORKSHIRE

ROOS   B1242   WITHERNSEA

?

NOT TO SCALE

A sketch, not to scale, of the probable layout of Thirtle Bridge Camp, as deduced from the remains in the 1950s. (Map courtesy of Stewart Hodgson, Mona House)

74

The bungalow, Mona House, much modernised, that was the Officers' Mess at Thirtle Bridge Camp.

Thirtle Bridge Cook House from the west, still standing in 2010.

Tunstall Drain, looking west, with Thirtle Bridge on the ridge in the middle distance. This is typical rolling Holderness countryside.

The only known picture of Thirtle Bridge Camp, taken in 1918, with four of the officers posing for the camera. (Image courtesy of the Sloan family).

"Erb, Allan, Pease Bill as we are known at Thirtle Bridge"

Headquarters Z Company, Lancashire Fusiliers. This photograph is almost certainly taken at Sand-le-Mere, where from June 16th 1916 Z Company had a base. It was an outpost of Thirtle Bridge Camp.
(Image courtesy of the Sloan family)

Tunstall Hall was the Headquarters of the 3rd Lancashire Fusiliers Humber Garrison at Thirtle Bridge. It was also used as officers' accommodation.

The submarine forest, Tunstall, a reminder of the ravages of the sea in times past. It is actually at Sand-le-Mere, and Tolkien's coastal lookout post would have been behind the camera, and to the right.

A scene from an old postcard c1900. The corner of Queen Street and Hull Road, Withernsea. 78 Queen Street was J Westerdale's shop and 76 Queen Street was the second bay window immediately behind it.

A modern view of the corner of Hull Road. 76 and 78 Queen Street have now been connected to make the Lifeboat Café. 76 Queen Street was where the white door is at the left hand side.

CONFIDENTIAL

PROCEEDINGS OF A MEDICAL BOARD   Army Form A. 45

assembled at Headquarters Humber Garrison, Hull.   on 16/11/17

by order of G.O.C. in C.H.G.(C.R.H.G. 79043)

for the purpose of examining and reporting upon the present state of health of

(Rank and Name) 2/Lt. J.R.R. Tolkien.

Age 25   Service 2 4/12   Disability French Fever. (Corps) 11th attch. S.Lan.Fus.

Date of commencement of leave granted for present disability.

Date on which placed on half-pay for present disability. 30-3-17.

The Board having assembled pursuant to order, and having read the instructions on the
back of the form, proceed to examine the above-named officer and find that
since leaving hospital 16-10-17 has had one slight attack
lasting 3 days, temp. only reaching 100.
He is slowly recovering his strength & looks much
better.

Instructions to Officer:- Foreman with 3 Lancs. Fus.

The Board will classify the officer under one of the following categories, the probable
period of unfitness for the higher categories being stated.

Fit for General Service... no.

Fit for Service in a Garrison or Labour Unit abroad.......... ✓

Fit for Home Service:-
    (1)   Active duty with troops.......................... Yes. 2 mos.
    (2)   Sedentary employment only...................... ✓

For admission to a Command Depot...........................

Requiring indoor Hospital treatment:-
    (1)   In an Officers' Military or Aux. Convl.Hospital...... ✓
    (2)   In an Officers' Hospital............................. ✓

Permanently unfit for any further Military Service............ ✓

7. In very special cases such as tuberculosis leave,
   not exceeding six months may be recommended by Medical Boards for special treatment, the Board giving detailed reasons for
   any such recommendation

8. Was the disability contracted in the service?.......... Yes

9. Was it contracted under circumstances over)
   which he had no control?   ) Yes

10. Was it caused by military service?.................... Yes

11. If caused by military service, to what)
    specific military conditions is it)   Infection on A.S.
    attributed?

12. If the disability was not caused by)
    military service, was it aggra-)
    vated thereby, and if so, by what)   ✓
    specific military conditions?

Officer's) H.Q. 3 Lancs Fus   Signature   H. Mingay.   President
Address   ) Thirtle Bridge   Member
) Withernsea   S.E.D. Granger   (R.T.O.)

MEDICAL BOARD REPORT ON A DISABLED OFFICER.
(ALSO TO BE USED FOR DISABLED NURSES.)

Army Form A. 45

1. Rank and Name.
2. Unit.
3. Age. 26
4. Address. HQ 9th RDC
6. Disability. Trench Fever
7. Date of origin of disability. Dec 1917
8. Place of origin of disability. Ancre - France.

Has had two attacks (slight) temperature reaching 100° necessitating... for 5 days.

Instructions to Officer:— To continue c̄ 9 RDC

OPINION OF THE MEDICAL BOARD.

10. Was the disability contracted (a) before entering the service? No
    (b) in the service? Yes
11. Was it attributable to military service? Yes
    If so, to what specific military conditions is it attributed? Superv... in a.d.

12. If not attributable to, was it aggravated by, military service?
    If so, by what specific military conditions?

13. Is it attributable to, or aggravated by, the officer's own negligence or misconduct? If so, in what way, and to what extent? No

[P.T.O.

Tolkien's medical report for January 19th 1918, with his address as the 9th R.D.C., Easington, where he was to remain for the time being.
(Courtesy of the National Archives, Kew)

Easington and Kilnsea

The Medical Board at the Humber Garrison, convened on November 16th 1917 (55), recommended that Tolkien stay with the 3rd Lancashire Fusiliers at Thirtle Bridge, but a surviving letter from Edith, dated November 19th 1917, is addressed to him at 9th Royal Defence Corps, Kilnsea. Coincidentally, Edith had given birth to a son, John Francis Reuel, at the Royal Nursing Home in Cheltenham on the same day as her husband's medical board. It was a difficult birth, and so JRRT managed to arrange a visit to see her in Cheltenham on November 22nd. During November, letters of congratulation on the birth of their first child were posted either to 2 Trinity Terrace, Cheltenham or to, once again, the 9th Royal Defence Corps, Kilnsea. Anyone knowing the area knew that this could only mean Godwin Battery, for there was precious little other military accommodation in the hamlet, and there were thousands of army personnel packed into this tiny corner of south east Holderness. The sender obviously assumed that the local postman would readily identify the correct address.

The Royal Defence Corps could be regarded as the Great War's equivalent of the Home Guard of the Second World War. Like the Home Guard, the men who formed it at its inception in 1916 were those too old for the regular army. Their numbers were strengthened by the subsequent addition of men who, like Tolkien, required 'hardening' before they returned to fighting overseas. There were 18 Royal Defence Corps Battalions formed from various other regiments. The 9th Battalion had formerly been the 1st (Home Service) Garrison Battalion Leicestershire Regiment (57). Their base was Easington, but it is clear that the men were also billeted at nearby Kilnsea. Two records exist of soldiers belonging to D Company of the 9th R.D.C. being billeted at number 3 and number 5 Hut, Kilnsea Camp (58). However, no-one knows where in Easington the 9th R.D.C. had their H.Q., for a number of houses and fields in the locality had been occupied by the military since earlier in the war. Fortunately, Robert Walker of Tower House, Easington, kept a diary throughout the conflict, and it is soon apparent from reading this, that the village was inundated with military personnel (59). In November 1914 it was the members of the 17th Battalion Northumberland Fusiliers that were billeted in his house and adjoining cottage. By April 1915, several units of various regiments had resided in the village and moved on. It was then the turn of the Lancashire Fusiliers, who camped in his home field, for more and more officers were asking Walker for the use of his properties and fields. He offered permission to the military authorities to occupy his home field and cottage premise free until peace was signed. There was a soldiers' concert in A field in December 1916, and by July 1917, B field was in use as a drilling and games area. All in all, it is apparent that the army had a major presence in the village. An interesting snippet from his diary, dated March 22nd 1918, records the passing of the R.D.C., for it curtly observes 'the Royal Defence

Corps disbanded and the East Yorkshires arrived.' Surely, Walker would not have recorded this fact for posterity if he had not been directly involved, hence I am confident that some, or all of his fields, cottages and barns were in use by them at the time of their disbandment. After the war, the auctioneers mentioned earlier with regard to the clearance of the Thirtle Bridge hutments, N Easton, were at work in Easington. On October 6th 1919, they auctioned off some of the military huts in A field. Unfortunately, this brings us no nearer to locating the site of the H.Q. of the R.D.C. What is known, is that while Tolkien was based at Easington, he had a major disagreement, by letter, with his fellow TCBS member, Christopher Luke Wiseman (60).

Moving on to Kilnsea, the major base called Godwin Battery was situated near the Bluebell Inn. The road east of the inn once led to Old Kilnsea, but the last vestiges of this settlement had been devoured by the sea in the 1850s. At first hand, JRRT would have witnessed the site of this lost village, under the waves down a road seeming to go nowhere - another reminder that the Holderness coast is a coast of lost villages. Construction on Godwin Battery had started earlier in the Great War, and it was a large site with gun placements, barracks, workshops and most important of all to Tolkien at this time, a hospital. The Proceedings of the Medical Board assembled at the Headquarters, Humber Garrison, Hull, on November 16th 1917 (61), had this directive on a slip pasted in. Under the heading 'Requiring indoor Hospital treatment', two boxes are ticked - 1) In an Officers' Military or Aux. Convl. Hospital, and 2) In an Officers' Hospital. The report notes that 'Since leaving Hospital 16 / 10 / 1917 has had one slight attack lasting 3 days, temp reaching 100°. He is slowly recovering his strength and looks much better'. It then proceeds to say that he was rated 20% disabled and unfit for general service for two months, but fit for home service for two months and is told to remain with the 3rd Lancashire Fusiliers at Thirtle Bridge. Despite this instruction, JRRT ended up at Easington late in November. I believe that after JRRT had left Brooklands Hospital in October, the autumn chills at Thirtle Bridge had probably slowed his recovery, and so they may have felt that some hospitalisation, albeit limited, would be beneficial, hence the move to Kilnsea with its hospital. One has to assume that there were not similar facilities at Thirtle Bridge. There is another possible reason for the move, which I suggest in the next paragraph. Despite any limited hospitalisation, Tolkien would still be available for the relatively light duties demanded of him by the 9th Royal Defence Corps at Easington. On January 19th 1918, the Medical Board had more to add. Tolkien, by now a full lieutenant 'Had had two attacks (slight) temperature reaching 100° - necessitating rest in bed for 5 days'. The report then adds 'On the whole he is gradually improving and feels much stronger'. By now, JRRT was considered to be 20% disabled, and ruled unfit for general service for one month, but fit for active duty with troops on home service for one month. He was told to continue with the

9th Royal Defence Corps at Easington, and what is significant in the light of the need for hospitalisation, the report stated 'he is receiving treatment from the regimental medical officer'.

Creatively what did happen at Easington and Kilnsea was that Tolkien found time to return to his mythology and rework the old opening of 'The Wanderer's Allegiance', which was to become 'The Song of Eriol', referring to the wandering mariner in 'The Book of Lost Tales'. There is a note that must have been added later to one of the manuscripts, that states 'Easington 1917–18' (62). A poem that he had started earlier in the war, 'The Lonely Harebell', resurfaced, and eventually became renamed 'Elf Alone'. As the latter, on the manuscript the author added a note – '1915 -1916 rewritten 1918 / Cromer / Hospital / Birmingham / Farmhouse near Easington, Yorks'. This cryptic scribble opens up a completely new dimension to JRRT's stay on the peninsula. There is no surviving correspondence between him and Edith from November 1917 to July 1918, so one can only speculate as to their whereabouts. However, the 1977 biography by Humphrey Carpenter states that, after giving birth to her son, Edith returned north to Roos, to be near her husband. It is highly unlikely that she would lodge at Roos, for it is a considerable distance from Easington, and transport between the villages was very poor indeed in the early 20th century. She knew that he had been posted to Easington, and if she did indeed come back to Yorkshire, she would have surely have sought accommodation south, not north of Withernsea, especially if he were billeted at Kilnsea, The references to Birmingham make some sense, especially with 'hospital' but the mention of 'Cromer' is unclear.

If he actually resided in a farmhouse, not the barracks at Godwin Battery, then it is possible that Edith and baby John managed to stay with him during early 1918. To pay for Edith's stay in a nursing home in November, he had sold the last of his patrimonial shares in the South African mines (63). Could it be that sufficient funds were left over to allow the family to be together for a short while at such an important family milestone for them? Additionally, it is surely strange that Tolkien's medical board, sitting on the same day that his wife gave birth, recommended that he return to Thirtle Bridge, and yet, at the end of November he had not returned to his old camp, but moved on to Easington. Certainly, his former establishment would have been more convenient for the train for Edith and baby John, being three miles from Withernsea station as opposed to at least seven from Patrington station to Easington. But balanced against this would be the opportunity for the family to lodge together, and for the author to still receive the hospital care dictated by the medical board of November 16th 1917. The difficult childbirth, the subsequent need for Edith to be cared for, and the possibility of being together as a family must surely have focused JRRT's mind to find a solution. Was the answer a 'farmhouse near Easington'? We do not know if all the local farmhouses took officers as lodgers, but there was considerable demand for accommodation in the locality with such an influx of soldiers. This is where Robert Walker's diary is able to provide assistance, for the entry for February 28th 1917 records the fact that 'Capt C.A.E. Chudleigh called about lodgings for his wife and child'. Here is primary evidence that it was possible for a military family to all reside together locally. They obviously stayed for a good while, for the diary notes on November 8th 1917, 'Capt & Mrs Chudleigh and child finally left Easington' (64). Wherever they stayed, could it be that within a month, the Chudleighs' place of residence was taken over by the writer and his family?

What we can be deduce, is that 'near Easington' almost certainly means between Easington and Kilnsea, where he had his postal address, and where he was receiving treatment. Even in 1918, the number of farmhouses on the mile and a half between the two villages was very limited. Travelling south along Easington Road towards Kilnsea, you first reach Firtholme Farm on the east side. Then, a mile further south on the same side, on the northern edge of Kilnsea is Kilnsea Grange (which was called Grange Farm then). You are now into the hamlet of Kilnsea, and Westmere Farm would have been followed by Blackmoor Farm, but this farmhouse has since gone. Cliff Farm is on the riverside, at the point where the road curves sharply away from the River Humber. You then pass St. Helen's Church on the left, and just beyond Godwin Battery, now on the road to Spurn Point, is Southfield Farm. Down South End, Easington, there was South End Farm, South Farm, Lockham Farm and Humberdale. Interestingly, Robert Walker sold off Lockham Farm in 1920, so he did actually own a farmhouse, which has since been demolished, between Easington and Kilnsea during the war years. Unfortunately, unless new evidence comes to light, at this distance in time I have been unable to deduce which farmhouse might have been the residence of the author in 1917 / 18.

Furthermore, it is possible that he did actually stay in Kilnsea itself. During the research for this book, I noticed that the military tended to be ambiguous about defining locations. This would probably be for security reasons, and, as an officer, Tolkien may have adopted a similar cautious approach to addresses in his correspondence. To give examples from military correspondence, I have observed that Hornsea Musketry Camp was actually at Rolston, and that the Lancashire Fusiliers Ottringham H.Q. was actually at Halsham. In fact, as noted earlier in the book, Tolkien himself described his stay at Thirtle Bridge Camp as being 'in a lonely house near Roos'. Was this ambiguity official policy, to create uncertainty as to the exact location of military establishments and personnel?

Of one thing you can be certain, staying at Kilnsea during the winter months would have exposed Tolkien to the raw sea mists and gales that sweep over the north eastern coast in this season. It would not have been difficult for him to imagine the ravaging hordes of earlier Germanic or Viking raiders appearing through the sea frets and riding over the surf to land on these exposed shores. The bleakness, and the consciousness of being on the very margin of land and sea, must surely have entered Tolkien's psyche, and underscored his separation from his heartland in the West Midlands.

On March 19th 1918, Tolkien was examined again (65), and the report of the Medical Board at the Humber Garrison stated 'An attack of influenza which confined him to bed for five days has delayed this officer's hardening'. The medical officer then adds 'His general tone is improving, but he still requires hardening. He is rated 20% disabled, unfit for general service, but fit for active duty with troops on home service, and therefore is instructed to continue with the 3rd Lancs. Fus. at Thirtle Bridge, where he is now no longer receiving any medical treatment.' The record that he is attached to the 9th Royal Defence Corps is deleted. This report seems to ignore the fact that at the time JRRT was actually at Easington, but does recognise that upon the disbanding of the 9th R.D.C., Tolkien would be returning to Thirtle Bridge once more.

Easington village today, looking west. All Saints' Church is on the left and the old coastguard house with the turret is opposite. The new village hall occupies the foreground.

On the road out of Easington towards Kilnsea is 'The Tower'. Originally called Mount Pleasant, by WW1 it was owned by Robert Walker, who kept a diary. At the time, the plinth in front of the house had an eagle on it, but anti-German feeling was so high that on April 15th 1916, Mr Walker took it down and smashed it!

The entrance to Sandy Beaches Camp at Kilnsea, the site of Godwin Battery. The site of the hospital that Tolkien would have attended is near this sign. The barracks were off to the right.

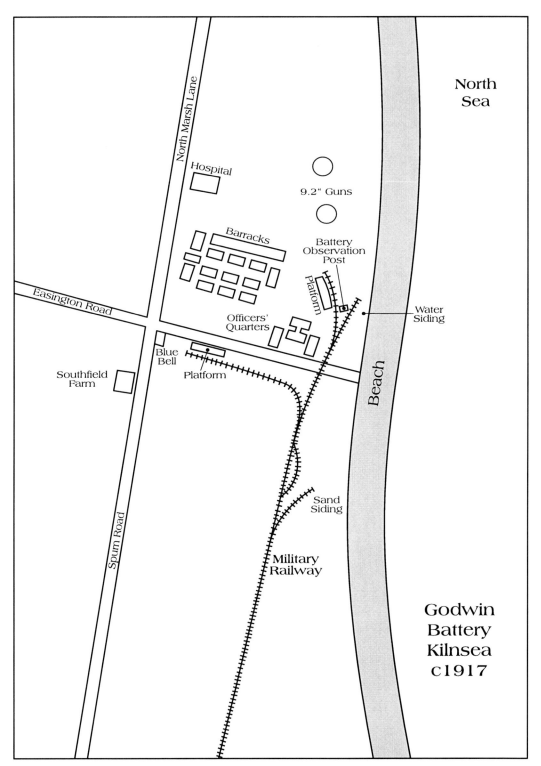

A sketch, not to scale, of the layout of Godwin Battery at Kilnsea in the Great War, as copied from aerial photographs of the time. (Map kindly drawn by Dave Shaw)

Conclusion

I hope that you have enjoyed your wanderings around East Yorkshire, from populous Kingston upon Hull, through the pleasant seaside resorts of Hornsea and Withernsea, and finally on to remote Kilnsea, in the extremity of southern Holderness. I have printed a separate chapter at the end that chronologically lists the events detailed above. I trust that the reader now has a clearer picture of Tolkien's period of residence in the area, and also a greater understanding of the influence that the region had on his burgeoning mythology. Yet mysteries remain. Where was Edith in June and early July 1917? If Edith did manage to stay with her husband, where exactly was it? Where did cousin Jennie Grove reside after leaving Harrogate in March 1917 and Hornsea in April and May 1917? Finally, did Edith and baby John manage to travel up and stay in Yorkshire in late 1917 / early 1918, and if so where did they lodge, and was JRRT able to reside with them?

There are other East Riding of Yorkshire connections which are outside the scope of this book. Firstly, Tolkien and his family holidayed in Filey, at the northern edge of the riding, while he was employed at Leeds University. The first occasion was in the summer of 1922, and the second time in late August / early September 1925, when there was a tremendous storm (66). The other local point of reference is Wetwang, on the

Yorkshire Wolds, a place name that appears in 'The Lord of the Rings'.

After Tolkien moved out of his home in Leeds and departed from Yorkshire in January 1926, he truly became a 'Middle-Englander' once more. His childhood roots had been in the Birmingham area, and most of his adult life was spent in Oxford. His wartime convalescence had introduced him to this coastline of legendary lost villages, but his future life lay in the populous heartland of England. Tolkien may have left the sea-mists and insubstantial coast of Holderness behind him physically, but at a critical time in his creative life, they had left a very substantial mark upon him.

Any research ultimately must be incomplete, for there is always a point at which no further details can be substantiated and the researcher departs into the realms of speculation. I hope in this small volume I have added to the store of knowledge about the writer who captured the imagination of so many readers around the world.

CHRONOLOGICAL OVERVIEW OF TOLKIEN'S STAY IN EAST YORKSHIRE

27 / 11 / 1916   ORDER FOR JRRT, WHEN READY, TO GO FROM EDGBASTON HOSPITAL TO 3RD RESERVE BATTALION LANCASHIRE FUSILIERS, THEN AT OTTRINGHAM (W.O. LETTER)

18 / 12 / 1916   CORRESPONDENCE (REF 1000054/2, A.G.4c) TO COMMANDING OFFICER 3RD LANCASHIRE FUSILIERS, TUNSTALL HALL, ABOUT JRRT BEING SENT TO HOLDERNESS (W.O. LETTER, DATED 21 / 4 /1917 BELOW)

28 / 3 / 1917   PROCEEDINGS OF MEDICAL BOARD, FURNESS AUXILIARY HOSPITAL, HARROGATE, DISABILITY LEAVE ORIGINALLY GRANTED 25 / 10 / 1916, MENTIONS 3RD BATTALION LANCASHIRE FUSILIERS AT WITHERNSEA, AND RECOMMENDS THREE WEEKS SICK LEAVE (W.O. LETTER)

18 / 4 / 1917   JRRT AND CHRISTOPHER LUKE WISEMAN HAVE 'COUNCIL OF HARROGATE'. SICK LEAVE FOR JRRT ENDS

19 / 4 / 1917   JRRT INITIALLY POSTED TO HORNSEA,
                  MUSKETRY CAMP
                  EDITH AND JENNY GROVE AT HORNSEA?
                  DATE OF JRRT JOINING 3RD RESERVE
                  BATTALION (SEE BELOW)

21 / 4 / 1917   LETTER FROM COMMANDING OFFICER, 3RD
                  LANCASHIRE FUSILIERS TUNSTALL HALL.
                  JRRT JOINED 3RD LANCASHIRE FUSILIERS ON
                  19 / 4 / 1917 (W.O. LETTER)

1 / 5 / 1917   PROCEEDINGS OF MEDICAL BOARD TO WAR
                  OFFICE (W.O. LETTER FROM HUMBER
                  GARRISON 130 ANLABY ROAD, HULL)

5 / 5 / 1917   LETTER FROM EDITH AT 1 BANK TERRACE,
                  HORNSEA, TO JRRT, NOW WITH 3RD BATTALION
                  LANCASHIRE FUSILIERS AT THIRTLE BRIDGE.
                  ONE LETTER OF SEVERAL FROM EDITH TO
                  JRRT IN MAY 1917, RE-DIRECTED TO
                  MUSKETRY CAMP, HORNSEA

12 / 5 / 1917   MEDICAL DOSSIER STATES JRRT FIT FOR
                  HOME SERVICE (W.O. LETTER)

12 / 5 / 1917   POSTCARD FROM EDITH AT 1 BANK TERRACE,
                  HORNSEA, TO JRRT AT THIRTLE BRIDGE,
                  REDIRECTED TO HORNSEA MUSKETRY CAMP

18 / 5 / 1917   ENVELOPE POSTMARKED ON THIS DATE
ADDRESSED TO JRRT, 1 BANK TERRACE,
HORNSEA

1 / 6 / 1917   PROCEEDINGS OF MEDICAL BOARD TO WAR
OFFICE (W.O. LETTER FROM HUMBER
GARRISON 130 ANLABY ROAD, HULL)

1 / 6 / 1917   LAST OF LETTERS FROM EDITH AT 1 BANK
TERRACE TO JRRT AT 3RD BATTALION
LANCASHIRE FUSILIERS, THIRTLE BRIDGE

2 / 6 / 1917   EDITH NO LONGER AT 1 BANK TERRACE
EDITH AT ROOS OR THIRTLE BRIDGE UNTIL
11 / 7 / 1917?

12 / 7 / 1917   LETTER FROM EDITH AT 76 QUEEN STREET,
WITHERNSEA TO JRRT AT 3RD BATTALION
LANCASHIRE FUSILIERS, THIRTLE BRIDGE

14 / 7 / 1917   LETTER FROM EDITH AT 76 QUEEN STREET,
WITHERNSEA RE-ADDRESSED FROM HORNSEA
MUSKETRY CAMP TO JRRT AT 'WAVERLEY',
CLIFF ROAD, HORNSEA

14 / 7 / 1917	LETTER FROM EDITH AT 76 QUEEN STREET, WITHERNSEA RE-ADDRESSED TO JRRT AT R.E. SIGNAL DEPOT, DUNSTABLE, BEDS
20 / 7 / 1917 to 25 / 7 / 1917	JRRT AT DUNSTABLE, FAILED SIGNALLING EXAM
21 / 7 / 1917	LETTER FROM EDITH AT 76 QUEEN STREET, WITHERNSEA TO JRRT AT R.E. SIGNAL DEPOT, DUNSTABLE, BEDS, RE-DIRECTED TO WITHERNSEA
1 / 8 / 1917	JRRT AND HUXTABLE AT ANNUAL MINDEN DAY DINNER, PROBABLY AT THIRTLE BRIDGE OR TUNSTALL HALL
13 / 8 / 1917	LETTERS UNTIL 21 / 8 FROM EDITH AT 76 QUEEN STREET, WITHERNSEA TO JRRT, BROOKLANDS OFFICERS' HOSPITAL, COTTINGHAM ROAD, HULL
21 / 8 / 1917	LAST OF LETTERS FROM EDITH AT 76 QUEEN STREET, WITHERNSEA TO JRRT IN BROOKLANDS HOSPITAL, COTTINGHAM ROAD, HULL

24 / 8 / 1917   LETTERS UNTIL 11 / 9 FROM EDITH AT 37 MONTPELLIER VILLAS, CHELTENHAM TO JRRT, BROOKLANDS OFFICERS' HOSPITAL, COTTINGHAM ROAD, HULL

11 / 9 / 1917   LAST OF LETTERS FROM EDITH AT 37 MONTPELLIER VILLAS, CHELTENHAM TO JRRT, BROOKLANDS OFFICERS' HOSPITAL, COTTINGHAM ROAD, HULL

12 / 9 /1917   LETTERS UNTIL 15 / 10 FROM EDITH AT 6 ROYAL WELL TERRACE, CHELTENHAM TO JRRT, BROOKLANDS OFFICERS' HOSPITAL, COTTINGHAM ROAD, HULL

15 / 10 / 1917   LAST OF LETTERS FROM EDITH AT 6 ROYAL WELL TERRACE, CHELTENHAM TO JRRT, BROOKLANDS OFFICERS' HOSPITAL, COTTINGHAM ROAD, HULL

16 / 10 / 1917   JRRT LEAVES BROOKLANDS OFFICERS' HOSPITAL, COTTINGHAM ROAD, HULL. HE IS RATED 30% DISABLED, BUT TOLD TO REJOIN 3RD LANCASHIRE FUSILIERS AT THIRTLE BRIDGE , AS FIT FOR LIGHT DUTIES (W.O. LETTER)

16 / 11 / 1917   PROCEEDINGS OF MEDICAL BOARD TO WAR
                  OFFICE WITH REPORT BELOW (W.O. LETTER
                  FROM HUMBER GARRISON 130 ANLABY ROAD,
                  HULL)

16 / 11 / 1917   MEDICAL BOARD REPORT H.Q. HUMBER
                  GARRISON, HULL. JRRT BASED AT THIRTLE
                  BRIDGE, TO REMAIN WITH 3RD LANCASHIRE
                  FUSILIERS THERE. MENTIONS THAT
                  ALTHOUGH JRRT WAS SLOWLY RECOVERING,
                  HE STILL REQUIRED INDOOR HOSPITAL
                  TREATMENT. HE IS CONSIDERED 20%
                  DISABLED. (W.O. LETTER)

16 / 11 / 1917   EDITH GIVES BIRTH TO JOHN FRANCIS REUEL.
                  LETTERS OF CONGRATULATIONS ON THE
                  BIRTH OF HIS FIRST CHILD ABOUT THIS TIME
                  ADDRESSED TO EITHER 2 TRINITY TERRACE,
                  CHELTENHAM OR TO 9TH ROYAL DEFENCE
                  CORPS, KILNSEA

19 / 11 / 1917   LETTER TO JRRT, 9TH ROYAL DEFENCE CORPS,
                  KILNSEA

24 / 11 / 1917   JRRT PROMOTED TO LIEUTENANT,
                  BACKDATED TO 1 / 7 / 1917

12 / 1917   EDITH AND BABY AT ROOS / EASINGTON?

19 / 1 / 1918   MEDICAL BOARD REPORT H.Q. HUMBER
GARRISON, HULL. JRRT TO REMAIN WITH 9TH
ROYAL DEFENCE CORPS AT EASINGTON. STILL
20% DISABLED, BUT FIT FOR ACTIVE SERVICE
WITH TROOPS ON HOME SERVICE. STILL
RECEIVING TREATMENT FROM THE
REGIMENTAL MEDICAL OFFICER (W.O. LETTER)

19 / 2 / 1918   PROCEEDINGS OF MEDICAL BOARD TO WAR
OFFICE. JRRT STILL BELOW PAR AND
REQUIRES HARDENING (W.O. LETTER FROM
HUMBER GARRISON 130 ANLABY ROAD, HULL)

16 / 3 / 1918   MACKERETH AT THIRTLE BRIDGE (W.O.
LETTER, NATIONAL ARCHIVE REF : 339 /
60159)

19 / 3 / 1918   MEDICAL BOARD REPORT H.Q. HUMBER
GARRISON, HULL. JRRT BASED AT THIRTLE
BRIDGE, TO CONTINUE WITH 3RD LANCASHIRE
FUSILIERS, AS INFLUENZA HAD DELAYED HIS
HARDENING (W.O. LETTER)

19 / 3 / 1918   JRRT RETURNS TO THIRTLE BRIDGE AFTER
DISBANDING OF ROYAL DEFENCE CORPS

10 / 4 / 1918   MEDICAL BOARD REPORT H.Q. HUMBER
GARRISON, HULL. STATES JRRT STILL AT
THIRTLE BRIDGE, HAS NOW RECOVERED AND
FIT FOR GENERAL SERVICE. TO CONTINUE
WITH 3RD LANCASHIRE FUSILIERS THERE (W.O.
LETTER)

10 / 4 /1918   JRRT TO PENKRIDGE CAMP, THEN SOON
AFTER TO BROCTON CAMP, CANNOCK CHASE

29 / 6 / 1918   JRRT BACK TO BROOKLANDS OFFICERS'
HOSPITAL, COTTINGHAM ROAD, HULL AFTER
CONTRACTING GASTRITIS

10 / 7 / 1918   LETTER FROM EDITH AT TEDDESLEY, NEAR
PENKRIDGE, STAFFS TO JRRT, 3RD
LANCASHIRE FUSILIERS, THIRTLE BRIDGE

12 / 7 /1918   LETTERS UNTIL 24 / 7 FROM EDITH AT
TEDDESLEY, NEAR PENKRIDGE, STAFFS TO
JRRT, BROOKLANDS OFFICERS' HOSPITAL,
COTTINGHAM ROAD, HULL

17 / 7 / 1918   PROCEEDINGS OF MEDICAL BOARD TO WAR
OFFICE (W.O. LETTER FROM HUMBER
GARRISON 130 ANLABY ROAD, HULL)

24 / 7 / 1918 LAST OF LETTERS FROM EDITH AT
TEDDESLEY TO JRRT AT BROOKLANDS
OFFICERS' HOSPITAL, COTTINGHAM ROAD,
HULL

25 / 7 / 1918 LETTERS UNTIL 7 / 8 FROM EDITH AT 1
BLENHEIM PARADE, PITTVILLE CHELTENHAM
TO JRRT AT BROOKLANDS OFFICERS'
HOSPITAL, COTTINGHAM ROAD, HULL

26 / 7 / 1918 ORDER FOR JRRT TO BE POSTED TO HIS
BATTALION AND PROCEED TO FRANCE VIA
BOULOGNE THE FOLLOWING DAY,
COUNTERMANDED ON 31 / 7

7 / 8 / 1918 LAST OF LETTERS FROM EDITH AT 1
BLENHEIM PARADE, PITTVILLE
CHELTENHAM TO JRRT AT BROOKLANDS
OFFICERS' HOSPITAL, COTTINGHAM ROAD,
HULL

10 / 8 / 1918 LETTERS UNTIL 9 / 9 FROM EDITH AT 2
TRINITY TERRACE, CHELTENHAM TO JRRT AT
BROOKLANDS OFFICERS' HOSPITAL,
COTTINGHAM ROAD, HULL

4 / 9 / 1918 PROCEEDINGS OF MEDICAL BOARD TO WAR
OFFICE (W.O. LETTER FROM HUMBER
GARRISON 130 ANLABY ROAD, HULL)

4 / 9 / 1918	MEDICAL BOARD REPORT H.Q. HUMBER GARRISON, HULL JRRT IN BROOKLANDS OFFICERS' HOSPITAL COTTINGHAM ROAD, HULL, AND TO REMAIN THERE UNTIL FURTHER ORDERS. HE HAD LOST NEARLY TWO STONE IN WEIGHT, AND WAS CONSIDERED 100% DISABLED AND UNFIT IN ANY CATEGORY FOR TWO MONTHS (W.O. LETTER)
8 / 9 / 1918	AMENDED PROCEEDINGS OF MEDICAL BOARD TO WAR OFFICE (W.O. LETTER FROM HUMBER GARRISON 130 ANLABY ROAD, HULL)
9 / 9 / 1918	LAST OF LETTERS FROM EDITH AT 2 TRINITY TERRACE, CHELTENHAM TO JRRT AT BROOKLANDS OFFICERS' HOSPITAL, COTTINGHAM ROAD, HULL. EDITH STILL AT 2 TRINITY TERRACE, CHELTENHAM
11 / 10 / 1918	JRRT LEAVES BROOKLANDS OFFICERS' HOSPITAL, COTTINGHAM ROAD, HULL FOR BLACKPOOL SAVOY CONVALESCENT HOSPITAL
19 / 11 / 1918	LETTER FROM EDITH AT 2 TRINITY TERRACE, CHELTENHAM TO JRRT AT 39 ST. JOHN STREET, OXFORD

Bibliography

Tolkien and the Great War – The Threshold of Middle-earth, John Garth, HarperCollins 2003
ISBN 9780007119523

The Tolkien Family Album, John & Priscilla Tolkien, HarperCollins 1992
ISBN 9780261102392

JRR Tolkien Companion and Guide, Christina Scull and Wayne G Hammond, HarperCollins 2006
ISBN 9780618391134

Kingston-upon-Hull before, during and after the Great War, Thomas Sheppard, A Brown & Sons 1919

Sisters of Mercy – Diocese of Middlesbrough 1857 - 2007

Hull & East Riding Graphic Newspaper

The Church of All Saints Roos – Historical notes

Holderness & Holdernessians, Fellow of the Royal Historical Society, Eastern Morning News, Hull 1878

The National Archives, Kew – W.O. 95 / 5459

The National Archives, Kew – W.O. 95 / 5460

The National Archives, Kew – W.O. 339 / 34423 (J R R Tolkien)

The National Archives, Kew – W.O. 339 / 60159 (Gilbert Mackereth)

The National Archives, Kew – W.O. 32 / 18622 (Royal Defence Corps)

Kelly's Local Directories – Hull & East Riding, various years 1893 – 1921

East Riding of Yorkshire Electoral Registers 1901 – 1947

National Censuses 1901, 1911, 1921

Crockford's Clerical Directories 1895 and 1926

Numerous Ordnance Survey maps between 1892 and the present

Lancashire Fusiliers Annuals for 1916, 1917 and 1918

References

Chapter 1

1) Tolkien and the Great War – The Threshold of Middle-earth, John Garth

2) The National Archives, Kew – W.O. 339 / 34423 (J R R Tolkien)

Chapter 2

3) The National Archives, Kew – W.O. 339 / 34423 (J R R Tolkien)

4) Kingston-upon-Hull before, during and after the Great War, Thomas Sheppard, p114 -115

5) Tolkien and the Great War – The Threshold of Middle-earth, John Garth, p240 & p241

6) Tolkien Family Papers, Bodleian Library, courtesy of the Tolkien Estate

7) The National Archives, Kew – W.O. 339 / 34423 (J R R Tolkien)

8) Tolkien and the Great War – The Threshold of Middle-earth, John Garth, p212 – 213 & p247

9) The National Archives, Kew – W.O. 339 / 34423 (J R R Tolkien)

10) Sisters of Mercy – Diocese of Middlesbrough 1857 – 2007

11) JRR Tolkien Companion and Guide, Christina Scull and Wayne G Hammond, p346 & 293 of the Chronology

12) The Institute of Our Lady of Mercy Archives, London

Chapter 3

13) Tolkien Family Papers, Bodleian Library, courtesy of the Tolkien Estate

14) 1916 Lancashire Fusiliers Annual, p304

15) The National Archives, Kew – W.O. 339 / 34423 (J R R Tolkien)

16) Tolkien Family Papers, Bodleian Library, courtesy of the Tolkien Estate

17) Hull & East Riding Graphic Newspaper (May 30th 1907)

18) www.thisishullandeastriding.co.uk

19) Tolkien Family Papers, Bodleian Library, courtesy of the Tolkien Estate

Chapter 4

20) Tolkien and the Great War – The Threshold of Middle-earth, John Garth, p238

21) The Church of All Saints Roos – Historical notes

22) The National Archives, Kew – W.O. 95 / 5459

23) Tolkien and the Great War – The Threshold of Middle-earth, John Garth, p237

24) JRR Tolkien Companion and Guide, Christina Scull and Wayne G Hammond, p100 of the Chronology

25) 1917 Lancashire Fusiliers Annual, p347 & 348

26) Crockford's Clerical Directories 1895 and 1926

27) Peter Cook, Withernsea

Chapter 5

28) The National Archives, Kew – W.O. 339 / 34423
(J R R Tolkien)

29) The National Archives, Kew – W.O. 95 / 5459

30) 1916 Lancashire Fusiliers Annual, p303

31) The Times, November 26th 1917

32) The National Archives, Kew – W.O. 339 / 34423
(J R R Tolkien)

33) Tolkien and the Great War – The Threshold of Middle-earth, John Garth, p245

34) Tolkien Family Papers, Bodleian Library, courtesy of the Tolkien Estate

35) Tony Simpson, Withernsea Lighthouse Museum

36) The Times, August 1st 1919

37) Tolkien and the Great War – The Threshold of Middle-earth, John Garth, p234 - 235

38) The National Archives, Kew – W.O. 339 / 60159
(Gilbert Mackereth)

39) 1918 Lancashire Fusiliers Annual, p366

40) Powys County Records Archive, County Hall, Lllandrindod Wells, LD1 5LG

41) Tolkien and the Great War – The Threshold of Middle-earth, John Garth, p236 - 237

42) Holderness & Holdernessians, p18 - 19

43) Tolkien Studies 4 – Walter E Haigh, Author of a New Glossary of the Huddersfield District, Janet Brennan Croft, 2007, p185

44) Tolkien and the Great War – The Threshold of Middle-earth, John Garth, p186

45) Tony Ellis, Tunstall Hall

46) 1917 Lancashire Fusiliers Annual, p341

47) JRR Tolkien Companion and Guide, Christina Scull and Wayne G Hammond, p101 of the Chronology

48) 1916 Lancashire Fusiliers Annual, p306

49) 1918 Lancashire Fusiliers Annual, p372

50) 1916 Lancashire Fusiliers Annual, p309

51) 1916 Lancashire Fusiliers Annual, p304

52) Tolkien Family Papers, Bodleian Library, courtesy of the Tolkien Estate

53) Tolkien and the Great War – The Threshold of Middle-earth, John Garth, p234

54) Tolkien Family Papers, Bodleian Library, courtesy of the Tolkien Estate

Chapter 6

55) The National Archives, Kew – W.O. 339 / 34423 (J R R Tolkien)

56) The National Archives, Kew – W.O. 32 / 18622 (Royal Defence Corps)

57) http://www.greatwarci.net/journals/30.pdf

58) http://1914-1918.invisionzone.com/forums/index.php?showtopic=159767

59) Robert Walker Diaries, Easington

60) Tolkien and the Great War – The Threshold of Middle-earth, John Garth, p251

61) The National Archives, Kew – W.O. 339 / 34423 (J R R Tolkien)

62) JRR Tolkien Companion and Guide, Christina Scull and Wayne G Hammond, p104 of the Chronology

63) Tolkien and the Great War – The Threshold of Middle-earth, John Garth, p242

64) Robert Walker Diaries, Easington

65) The National Archives, Kew – W.O. 339 / 34423 (J R R Tolkien)

Chapter 7

66) JRR Tolkien Companion and Guide, Christina Scull and Wayne G Hammond, p118 - 135 of the Chronology

Lightning Source UK Ltd.
Milton Keynes UK
UKOW010751200312

189264UK00001B/3/P